PLAYING TO LEARN

PLAYING TO LEARN

The Young Child, the Teacher and the Classroom

By

OTTO WEININGER, Ph.D.

Department of Applied Psychology
Ontario Institute for Studies in Education
University of Toronto
Toronto, Canada

and

SUSAN DANIEL, M.Ed.

North York Board of Education
North York, Ontario, Canada

CHARLES C THOMAS • PUBLISHER
Springfield • Illinois • U.S.A.

Published and Distributed Throughout the World by

CHARLES C THOMAS • PUBLISHER
2600 South First Street
Springfield, Illinois 62794-9265

© *1992 by* CHARLES C THOMAS • PUBLISHER

ISBN 0-398-05771-0

Library of Congress Catalog Card Number: 91-40974

With THOMAS BOOKS *careful attention is given to all details of manufacturing
and design. It is the Publisher's desire to present books that are satisfactory as to
their physical qualities and artistic possibilities and appropriate for their particular
use.* THOMAS BOOKS *will be true to those laws of quality that assure a good
name and good will.*

Printed in the United States of America
SC-R-3

Library of Congress Cataloging-in-Publication Data

Weininger, Otto, 1929–
    Playing to learn : the young child, the teacher, and the classroom
/ by Otto Weinginer and Susan Daniel.
        p. cm.
    Includes bibliographical references (p.   ) and index.
    ISBN 0-398-05771-0
    1. Play. 2. Learning. 3. Teaching. 4. Children—Language.
5. Child development. I. Daniel, Susan, M. Ed. II. Title.
LB1137.W45 1992
155.4'18—dc20   91-40974
                                                                        CIP

ABOUT THE AUTHORS

Dr. Otto Weininger is a full Professor of Educational Theory at the University of Toronto, teaching Clinical Child Psychology in the Department of Applied Psychology of The Ontario Institute for Studies in Education. Otto received his honours degree in Psychology from McGill University, Montreal, and his Ph.D. from the University of Toronto; his general field of inquiry since then has been the effects of early experience on later behavior and personality development. Over the years he has taught, consulted, and developed psychoanalytic play therapy programs in many settings concerned with child development: The Tavistock Institute in London, England; the Eliot-Pearson Department of Child Study at Tufts University in Massachusetts; the Child Study Centre at the University of British Columbia in Vancouver, and, in Toronto, in a residential treatment centre for emotionally disturbed children, at the Bloorview Crippled Childrens Centre; and in the Madison Avenue School, which he was instrumental in founding and for which he worked as a consultant and therapist for nearly ten years.

Dr. Weininger has received awards from Project Innovation, in California; the Ontario Confederation of University Faculty Associations, and the Ontario Psychological Association. He is a former editor of the *Journal of the Canadian Association for Young Children,* and presently editor of *Melanie Klein and Object Relations* and the *International Journal of Early Childhood.* In addition, Otto has published many articles dealing with such topics as readiness, play, personality development, neuropsychological and treatment models for emotionally disturbed children, school psychology, and maternal separation. His books include *Play and Education: The Basic Tool for Early Childhood Learning* (1979); *Out of the Minds of Babes: The Strength of Children's Feelings* (1982); *The Clinical Psychology of Melanie Klein* (1984); *The Differential Diagnostic Technique — A Visual Motor Projective Test* (1986), all published by Charles C Thomas, Publisher; and *Children's Phantasies: The Shaping of Relationships* (1989, Karnac Ltd., England).

Susan Daniel is the head of the Dramatic Arts Department at Downsview Secondary School in North York, Ontario. Raised in Chicago, Illinois and Madison, Wisconsin, she graduated in Speech and English from the University of Wisconsin and studied English Literature and History for a year at Edinburgh University. Sue toured with the Edinburgh Dramatic Society before returning to Wisconsin, where she worked variously as a recreation leader at a state training school for girls; as a director, designer, and playwright with Stagecoach Players, a touring teenage summer theatre group; and as a high school English and special education teacher, before immigration to Canada. As a child care worker in an Ontario residential treatment centre for emotionally disturbed children, she met Otto Weininger and became interested in continuing studies in psychology.

Sue began an informal and continuing partnership with Otto as a researcher and editor while staying home with her two young children; returning simultaneously to teaching and graduate school, she received her M.Ed. in Sociology and Psychology from the Ontario Institute for Studies in Education at the University of Toronto. In nearly 20 years with the North York Board of Education (one of the five public Metro Toronto boards) she has taught elementary school behavioral classes, junior high school special education, English as a Second Language, language arts, family studies, dramatic arts and guidance, and English and drama at the secondary level. An experienced writer of curricula in English and Dramatic Arts, Sue has also written many plays with and for children and adolescents, and has recently been heavily involved in several innovative arts education projects at the Faywood Arts Centre in the North York board and with the Ontario Arts Council.

INTRODUCTION

Currently, education is suffering from an inevitable backlash in public opinion. Over the last three decades schooling has been proclaimed as *the* answer to the world's woes, the equalizer and stabilizer of fragmented industrial societies as well as the modernizer of underprivileged agrarian societies, the stimulant for the masses and the tranquilizer for the radical few. With little or no help from anyone, the schools were expected to take every child, regardless of potential, home background, emotional stability, and motivation, and turn him into an educated, skilled, aware, sensitive and literate adult. That such an expectation would be unrealized was obvious at the start to those engaged in the actual process of education itself, but they were too overpowered by the hyperbole of idealistic, philosophical, and often political verbiage. In any case, soldiers in the midst of a battle are seldom consulted by the generals about long range plans for the war. What no one seemed to foresee was that ordinary people—parents, children, employers, and even some teachers—would react in justifiable anger against the schools when such promises were not fulfilled, society's problems were not all solved, and children were not all made whole as well as uniformly literate at an advanced level.

Statistics which show that today's students read as well as those two or three decades ago are ignored by media and parents alike. Much is made of the secondary school drop-out rate, yet, viewed historically, far more students stay in school—and graduate—than did those of their parents' generation. Students entering post-secondary institutions today do not, according to their professors, have the same skills levels as the university entrants of 1950; probably not, since in 1950 perhaps the top 5-10 percent of students went on to college or university, compared to nearly 50 percent in many countries today. One suspects, in fact, that if *only* the top 5 percent of today were considered, they would be found to be far better prepared, more knowledgeable, than the top 5 percent of 25 years ago.

Another factor is parental recognition of a reality which is particularly painful for any authority to acknowledge. Even 30 years ago parents knew everything their child would learn in school, and could, if necessary, simply impart all their knowledge of reading, writing, arithmetic, spelling, and the world to their children, who would then be adequately prepared for their own adult rôles. This is no longer true. Many parents sense that the new math, foreign language learning, economics, anthropology and so forth, which are part of current high school curricula, are beyond their ken. The occupations for which their children are being prepared are foreign both in name and in substance. They are no longer totally adequate guides for their children; even the structuring of the school system into credits, options, and pre-requisites foils their desire to be involved in planning their children's learning. Resultant feelings of inadequacy seldom find an outlet other than in anger and rejection.

A third factor is one which is perhaps a by-product of specialization and expertise. Many parents today feel totally unsure about the entire process of parenting. In the "good old days" you raised your children the way you were raised and thought little about it; common sense provided the solutions to most problems. Admittedly this system had drawbacks, especially for children with particular emotional, physical, or learning problems, but for the majority it worked. Bombarded by experts with theories on discipline, learning, toilet training and just about every other area of human existence, backed by piles of research, masses of statistics, and tons of degrees in fields most people don't even know exist, it is no wonder many parents are confused about how to be parents. It would be bad enough even if the experts always agreed, but this is never the case; a quick thought backwards at just one area — language learning — reminds us of the multiplicity of view which have been espoused over the years, often quite heatedly! The proliferation in middle class neighborhoods of study groups, panel discussions, and courses on various theories of child development is evidence of this gnawing insecurity about what is best for children. Thus it is doubly disappointing for parents when the school system, with experts by the dozens, research by the truckload, theories by the million can't guarantee success with their child any more than they can themselves.

This feeling of outrage is perhaps heightened by the pressures of economic life on most families. Uncertainty about their child-raising ability is increased by the necessity for parents to work, both in the majority of two-parent families, and in the vastly increased number of single-parent families. Guilt about the abandonment of time spent with children to the television sets of the nation (current estimates are that children spend about 12,000 hours in school by the age of 18, about 18,000 hours in front of the T.V.) is exacerbated by the knowledge that they have largely abandoned their children to the ministrations of the school as the sole place for learning about the world besides the T.V. set. It is always easier and more comfortable to look elsewhere for places to cast the blame than to examine one's own contribution to the problem. Even the knowledge that they did what they did because of economic necessity and a real belief that the school (and, by extension, the government), knows best does not mitigate the guilt and disappointment felt by many parents today.

Much of the guilt, rage, frustration and disappointment currently engulfing education centers around language—reading, writing, spelling, talking, bilingualism—because, and quite rightly, language is perceived by many as the most essential tool in man's repertoire. We have an awareness of not only the communicative but also the psychological and emotional necessity for language. We are always talking of subsequent layers of learning about language: from the mother and child's first sound, gesture, and expression "discussion"; to the pre-school and primary child's explorations of his world through play and consolidations of his discoveries through words; to the complicated question of the effects of bilingualism on the child's whole emotional, cultural, and social life; to the discovery of what "readiness to read" means for a particular child. One thing is clear. Given minimum levels of stimulation, most children will learn to talk, to think, to read, even to learn a second language—without much help and/or interference by the school system at all. It is perhaps indicative of our highly specialized, urbanized, pressurized society that we feel the need to maximize this learning in an attempt to protect our children from what we believe to be the chief hazards of adult life in this society—boredom, unhappiness, poverty, insecurity, and the feeling of being irrelevant, ineffective cogs in a highly complex, rapidly moving and very confusing machine. Quite accurately we recognize that problems with language exacerbate problems of transition from the secure safety of the very early environment to the lesser safety of the school, to the competitive and mind boggling dangers of the larger society. We seek to arm our children more effectively than we ourselves were armed to face a world whose complexities are defeating us and will just as surely, we fear, devastate our children.

But the answer does not really lie in what methods we use to teach reading, what standardized tests we apply to measure success—the real power of language lies in its ability to transmit feelings, needs, ideas, and beliefs from one person to another. The potential richness and satisfaction of language learning of whatever kind, at whatever level, is measured by ability to bridge the gap between two people by a word which joins them for a moment in a communal knowing-about.

For parents wondering what to do at home with their children to prepare them for school, the key to optimum language development continues to be what it has been since the dawn of man—sharing feelings, playing, talking, cuddling, exploring, laughing and crying together— being a family. Language development does not really have anything to do with expensive educational toys, private lessons, fancy vacations, and colour television. It has to do with time spent communicating the connectedness of the family as a unit in a wide variety of ways. It has to do with passing on ways of understanding and dealing with the world which reflect particular religious, philosophical and moral beliefs. It has to do with expectations, stimulations and challenges to the growing child's intellect. It has to do with communicating feelings about the worth of each child as a human being, recognition that everyone in the family has responsibilities, privileges, needs, feelings—and that this is true in the world outside the home too.

Basic to creating a family and nurturing children is the recognition that children learn so much of what they know while they live at home, not through rote memory with grades for passing and failing, but through playing, sharing, and trusting, through relationships with caring and guiding adults, through their own intrinsic desire to learn, to master the world around them, to communicate. These are also basic to building a validating educational experience in schools. This does not mean a laissez faire, permissive classroom. It does mean the necessity for a thorough knowledge of child development—emotionally, linguistically, conceptually, psychologically, socially. It does mean an ability to tune in to individual children's needs within the structure provided for an entire class. It does mean combining empathy with imagination, flair, a sense of humour, and academic competence. It does mean recognizing the differences in learning style, potential, and family background and organizing the classroom atmosphere appropriately.

The "basics" at school, then, are the same as the "basics" of common sense family life. Children learn through playing, through relationships with adults and peers because of intrinsic motivational factors which the good-enough teacher, like the good-enough parents, learns to utilize to the child's best advantage. Language and playing, language and thinking, language and learning—they are intertwined, connected, natural parts of living and growing. We cannot "make" a child talk more, learn faster, read with greater comprehension—any more than we can "make" a plant alter its patterns and produce different flowers. We can, through negligence, arrest growth, or we can, with care, provide a fertile environment and protect the growing plant from dangers and thus ensure maximum growth. As parents and teachers and educators, guardians of children entering the new world of words, our major goal must be to provide the atmosphere, to manipulate the environment, to stimulate the development and to nurture the minds and souls in such a way that children grow into a joyful competency and delight with their language. Only thus will they be able to truly communicate their humanity, both through their individuality and through their membership in the human family.

The following chapters represent a view that has evolved during the past 20 years. During those years both of us have continually worked with children, parents, and teachers and the discoveries of teaching and learning brought into focus in this book are as valid today as they were two decades ago.

CONTENTS

PLAYING TO LEARN

PART ONE
THE TEACHER, THE CHILD,
THE SCHOOL—FINDING AN IDENTITY

There was once a time when the process of education was considered a relatively straightforward thing; parents sent their children off to school and it was up to their teachers to teach them everything that was needed to succeed in the world. For the most part, we generally accepted the fact that some children would learn while others would not. It was all thought to be part of the educational process. However, the rapid changes in today's society have forced the realization that a proper education consists of more than just sending children to school for 7–8 hours a day and leaving the rest to harried and overworked teachers. Moreover, those things once synonymous with getting a good education such as learning the 3 R's and the memorization of names and dates are not sufficient for today's children and tomorrow's adults.

The four chapters in Part One of this book (Chapters 1 to 4) focus on the theme of education in terms of what it once was, what it now is, and what it must become if today's schools are to cope with the demands of the future. Chapter One deals with the role of the teacher in an ever changing society. Chapter Two addresses some of the important issues regarding the education of young children. Chapter Three discusses the complex problem of class size. Chapter Four outlines some of the ways in which the educational system must change in order to adequately prepare children for the future.

Chapter 1

TO BE A TEACHER

Once upon a time, not so very long ago, in a world less complex and more predictable than ours, teachers had a clear role to play in the education of the young. They were to impart skills, such as reading, writing, spelling and math, and they were to dole out facts and measure by examinations the ability of children to learn them. By their behaviour and language, through the discipline of their classrooms, they were also to reinforce the accepted values of the social system among the usually homogeneous group of children with whom they worked.

Although not an easy task for young teachers just out of Normal School, especially in the rural one-room setting, teaching was a task for which their entire early lives as "learners" adequately prepared them. They were the best "learners," the highest scoring examination-takers, and their teacher training provided them with more facts, some methods, some materials, then returned them to classrooms very like those they had left, in honour, such a short time before. From one decade to another, the facts they imparted changed only slightly—new dates at the end of the history curriculum, new names of famous people to memorize. They were preparing children to enter a world which changed slowly and whose landscapes were quite familiar. The future adult roles in the communities which the graduates were to fill were those they now saw filled by the adults of their collective families; and the linkage between generations, the connections between families over the years, made the transition to adulthood relatively simple.

It was not the school's place nor the teacher's role to prepare students for jobs—that role belonged to the parents and to the craftsmen of the community. The teacher's job was only to provide basic skills and accepted facts; and often these were only incidental to adult roles and jobs. It was the transmission of literacy and of the myths and values of the culture which the teacher's presence ensured. The occasional child who learned eagerly and well, who thrived on digesting information, who read widely all that was available and dreamed of other worlds, was destined for the

5

teacher training school, or the ministry, or the town newspaper, or, very
rarely, for the distant university. It was a simpler age, one which is long
gone in large urban communities, and which, though still superficially
present in some rural areas has rapidly retreated in the face of the
massive technological changes and social upheavals of the past fifty
years.

The changes in our society have, quite reasonably, brought changed
expectations of the school and the teacher's role in the education of
children. What is not so reasonable is the direction and scope of these
new expectations; all the *old* expectations—the teaching of basic skills
and accepted facts, the reinforcing of social values and discipline—are
still there. But by the widening of the world alone, especially in the great
influx of cultures, languages, and values, teaching just these "simple, old
fashioned things" is a much larger task. Added to this traditional
assignment, a hodge-podge of other tasks has fallen to the responsibility
of the school as they are abandoned by other institutions of society, or as
families are less able to perform what are basically socialization tasks.

The selection of children's eventual careers, or the vocations they will
be encouraged to choose from, now hinges on the school's assessment of
students' capabilities. A far wider range of technological vocations than
ever before has led to specialization in learning at ever earlier ages and
to a much wider selection of courses, such as data processing, auto
mechanics and drafting. The "new" disciplines of anthropology, sociology,
psychology and political science push more "information to be learned"
down into the high schools; the separation of the arts from the lives of
most working adults leaves the provision of training in and exposure to
music, art and theatre as the responsibility of the school. Working
mothers and the absence of the continuity of generations, of available
aunts, grandmothers and uncles to teach familiar domestic skills, puts
home economics and shop skills into the school curriculum. The discomfort of family members isolated from one another and from traditional religious values pushes sex and values education into the schools;
the largely non-physically active lifestyle of many urban children makes
physical education more necessary. The push of an increasingly multicultural society makes coping with the resulting tensions and values
clashes a major task of the school as a mini-social system; the threat, for
example, to Canada's national future makes the teaching of French a
priority, while the reality of increased immigration in many countries

makes teaching the native tongue as a second language an absolute necessity.

Most obviously, the seeming disintegration of modern society—reflected in the apathy of the adult population, the non-involvement of individuals with each other outside the nuclear family (and sometimes within it), the increase in violence and crime, the rising divorce rates and subsequent increase in single parent families, the sensationalism and blatant sexuality of the mass media, the soaring unemployment and inflation statistics, the racial and ethnic conflicts, the political non-involvement and cynicism of most adults—frightens people. And in their fears for themselves and their children they shift to the schools the burden of preparing children to cope with what their parents cannot, and call it "life skills education." In addition, the schools are often expected to detect and somehow remedy problems such as child abuse, depression, poverty and hunger, family alcoholism or drug abuse, juvenile crime and vandalism, learning disabilities, and emotional disturbances which have roots deep in the social malaise of the last decade of the twentieth century.

This wide range of knowledge which must be taught, the skills which must be imparted, the attitudes which must be ingrained or changed, are now the responsibility of the teacher. What was once gained from the family, the extended family, the school, the community and the church—speaking with almost one voice to the child—is now by default the responsibility of the school. And not only must the school, says society, teach about yesterday and train for today, it must also prepare for tomorrows which none of us can really predict.

A superhuman task—one which would tax all of us working with wisdom together—is abandoned to the lonely figure of the classroom teacher, who couldn't possibly succeed and will only be castigated for his or her failures by all the segments of society outside the school. Little wonder that teachers become so rapidly disillusioned, so quickly defensive, and that so many retreat to the safety of "read pp. 115–125 and do questions 1–10; quiz on Friday" or to concern about hours worked and money received. Most entered teaching when it was a far simpler task, expecting to be what their own teachers were—imparters of skills and information in a virtually closed system, caring about 'their' kids but responsible only for their academic learning, not for their emotional well-being, their future jobs, their social adjustment, their physical development, their social consciousness and their moral and ethical growth.

When most practising teachers entered their first classrooms, they expected to be admired, respected members of the community, to be satisfied, as they watched each year's class march out, that they had equipped their graduates with what was needed to compete in society. Most teachers are now suffering from what can best be described as acute culture shock coupled with desperate frustration and bitterness. The job they saw and were drawn to, as students, and were prepared for, in theory, by university and teacher training, is gone; in its place are expectations often beyond the ability of the total society, much less individuals, to meet successfully. And somehow their inability to meet these unfair expectations is *their* fault, and they have become society's scapegoat for its own failure to provide a meaningful and safe context for the growth and development of its children.

Through all this, the teacher training institutions continue to "prepare" young people to teach in a manner which only guarantees their failure by assuming that "more facts, some methods, and some materials" will still equip them to teach. WHAT could possibly prepare them to be amateur social workers, counsellors, therapists, vocational selectors, job placement agencies, surrogate parents, sex educators, values clarification experts, bureaucracy battlers, unbiased models for a multicultural society, referees of constant aggression, and entertainers who can compete against TV and films?

It seems obvious to us that it is time to critically evaluate the tasks which have been left to the teacher and the school. Only through a close analysis of the philosophies currently underlying our public educational system can we begin to pare down to manageable size the goals and expectations we place on teachers. It is only when teachers are less bombarded by the impossible, when society recognizes that its dissatisfaction with "the schools" has to do with the enormous variety of complex tasks now assigned to them, that teachers can begin to function coherently and with some measure of success again.

If it is not possible—and we suspect it is not—to divest schools of the enormous social responsibilities which they now carry, then at the very least it is necessary to begin to train people to work in a variety of roles within the schools—not as consultants, but in direct daily contact with children: as psychologists, as child care workers, as family therapists, as vocational skills trainers, as mental health workers, as ESL experts, as social workers, as recreation specialists—and let the person who wants to *teach* concentrate on a more finite and thus perhaps achievable task. The next step would then be to define the teacher's role in a more flexible way, not simply to advocate a return to the basics, the "memorize and regurgitate" facts to show you have learned the skills' way. This lock-step progression in education by which most of us were raised quite possibly accounts in part for our inability as an adult society to cope with constant change successfully.

It *is* possible to impart skills and facts in such a way that children learn to question, not just to accept; to encourage divergent thinking, not just one right answer for every question; to recognize that truth is a changing concept, even in disciplines such as history and science. Stripped of the necessity of being *everything to every* child, perhaps teachers would have the energy, both emotional and intellectual, to learn to teach in ways by which they generally were *not* taught themselves. In the past, children who questioned information, and thus authority, were not generally successful in the classroom; and teachers have spent a disproportionate share of their lives in classrooms, learning early not to question when the price was disapproval and/or academic failure.

Teacher training institutions perpetuated this same "one right way" system—the student who was most successful, and who could expect to get the "best" teaching job, with the finest references, was generally the one who accepted, or appeared to accept, the professor's model of teaching most wholly. Since most students in teacher training institutions had very little chance to practise alternative methods of teaching for large chunks of time in varying circumstances, they were not generally in a position to recognize before they began to teach how personal and individual a teaching style is, and how basically non-learnable or non-transferable is the unmeasurable but key factor of teacher-student personal interaction. The method of their favourite high school teacher was often stuck in their minds as the model of what they hoped to be in the classroom. Since so much of their learning about teaching was as learners in yet another classroom presided over by yet another expert, it is not unexpected that certain rigidities in methods, and a reluctance born of fear and unfamiliarity to try other ways, would manifest themselves when they began to teach.

Teacher training has not, then, tended to provide much that is useful in helping fledgling teachers make the transition from the ways they learned to some new ways of teaching. It passes on old methods and teaches new techniques based on the same old assumptions about the optimal way to learn. Chief among these is the idea that the teacher's major task is to master the specifics of skills so as to provide this information to the students in the classroom. This "specialization of skill" teaching in order to foster learning is usually given to the students in tidy instructional units to ensure measurable results and thereby demonstrate the proficiency of the teacher, and in retrospect, the value of his or her training. Gone is the clear recognition of all university students that work is to be done, tested, and then immediately forgotten. Microteaching, simulator teaching, programmed learning, and skills specialization are techniques based on our computer age philosophy, suggesting that that which can be mastered by measured amounts can be fed back by students in similarly measured amounts.

The pressures of our technological age have made teachers and those who teach them so anxious to quantify our instructional procedures and to measure the results that vast areas of information which do not lend themselves easily to such quantification are omitted. From this curriculum future teachers are taught token systems, interactional analysis and behaviour modification, but not so often ways to be aware of social dynamics and to cope with the political realities of the educational institution; to understand the conflict of interest between ideas taught in school and the personal and social attitudes students bring from home and view as "truth"; to focus on the conversation between student and teacher which is the foundation for learning and change; to consider the results of teaching methods upon the developing student's image of himself; or to be able to present information so that it is acceptable to people of different cultures without creating for these children a mistrust of their own culture or that of the majority culture. They are not taught what seems to us to be the basic, implicit recognition on the teacher's part that "Although I am talking to you in this way, providing this kind of information for you, it does not mean that there are not other ways of thinking and talking about this, or that your own ideas coming from your family and culture may not only enrich my ideas and information but may, in fact, give me another way to look at the world."

Another area which the "new" teaching methods obscure or relegate to unimportance is the arts, because they do not seem to fit into the scientific teaching method and cannot easily be provided with the lockstep system which is so frequently seen for math and science. So teachers pass on the message that the arts are less important, not entirely necessary in our society. All you have to do is listen to the elementary teacher who says, "Now children, after you have finished your math workbooks, you can draw until recess," or, worse still, "If you are all quiet for the next period and we have nothing left to do, we'll sing a few songs." Surely this attitude helps the young child to "realize" that art and music are unimportant time-fillers.

But in later school years, how does this influence the student's choice or valuing of those humanities subjects at the core of Western culture, such as history, classics, philosophy, literature and drama, and related "people" studies such as sociology, psychology, anthropology and politics? It seems that teachers suggest that this information is less important sometimes because they know too little about it, having been narrowly specialized themselves for too long; and because it is so much more difficult to teach since it needs to be thought and talked about, the kind of creativity it encourages is hard to measure, and the expertise involved centers on ideas, values, and cultural context, not just information. Thus less opportunity is offered to the student to recognize the society he lives in, or to examine it, or to understand dislocations of peoples of different cultures from the host culture. In other words, the seeds of rigidity, prejudice and technocracy may be sown by not stressing the arts as being as important to human development as are the sciences.

Perhaps the student revolts of the 60's and the early 70's were an attempt to avoid these rigidities, or maybe they were an expression of dissatisfaction with the limitations of the classroom experience. There are those who feel that the questions posed by teachers led to revolts; however, we don't think that this is what happened. Rather, the rigidities of our educational institutions created a feeling of alienation among students; this was then expressed as revolt. Students' dissatisfaction with not being able to understand the complete compartmentalization of learning, the "just learn this and give it back on the exam" way in which they were being taught, and their sense of isolation created by the rigid roles of teacher as "one who knows" and student as "one who doesn't know" forced, to a large extent, the confrontations and violent scenes of the period in the universities.

The dangers of continuing to impart in teacher training institutions methods which increase rigidity and decrease flexibility have been amply demonstrated, then, by students and teachers alike in the past two decades. The societal pressures on the schools and on teachers, so severe to begin with, have not been offset by the ways in which we train (and select, but that is another matter) young people to teach. We have kept the worst parts of the teacher/learner dichotomy in teacher training and added the worst parts of the push to quantify and make "scientific" both what we learn and how we teach. In so doing we have widened the gap, present at least since John Dewey (1938) articulated it, between those, classically educated, who see education as a raising of social consciousness and a source of positive change in the next generation, and those dedicated technologists who require only social preservation of the existing system and continuing fodder for the technological revolution.

Teacher training *must* become more effective, since it is the crucial transition from the unconsciously internalized methods by which teachers as students have been taught themselves, to more conscious, deliberate methods which might make the new teacher more responsive to the real needs of students today. This process is complicated by the realities of the recent years of teacher surplus, followed by the impending shortage of new teachers which is expected to last well into the 1990's as the late-breeding baby boomers' children reach the schools. For some years now, many schools have been staffed by teachers whose average age was 40+; now, suddenly, there will be an influx of very young teachers—with an entire generation missing in between the two groups. Will the traditional "mentoring" of brand new teachers, usually done by those who arrived a year or two earlier, the "new veterans," continue, or is this gap, the same width as that between these new teachers and their own parents in many cases, too wide to bridge? Will the waves of idealistic young teachers be left to sort it out on their own while their tired, often cynical elders watch—and wait to retire?

Perhaps, then, two kinds of teacher training are going to have to exist side by side; one for the new, inexperienced teacher and a parallel re-education for those already in teaching. This latter will be a mammoth undertaking, since, professionally, most experienced teachers are reluctant to change. They have set patterns and habits built up over the years to make their jobs as bearable under internal and external pressures as possible, and they are emotionally so demoralized by their perceived failure to meet the expectations of society and by the intense criticism they receive that, often defensive, cynical, and bitter, they are hardly fertile ground for retraining.

That is why the first step *must* be some societal understanding of the impossible complexity of the demands placed on teachers and schools, followed by a scaling down to feasible human capabilities of the role of the teacher. If, after examination, it is felt that schools must continue to bear such major responsibilities in the socialization, mental health, and job training areas, other professionals should be trained to fill some of the multi-roles now expected of the classroom teacher.

Given a contraction of the teacher's role in child development and learning, what, then, would we want to train teachers, old and new, to do in classrooms? What skills, what techniques, what information do they need? What attitudes or mind sets or personality traits must be cultivated, what understandings reached, in order to be effective in what would still be a group of students with a multitude of different backgrounds and a wider variety of needs in an increasingly complex society? What, then, *should* teachers be doing in classrooms?

Developing answers in depth to these questions could occupy the time and energies of classroom teachers, parents, administrators, and professionals in teacher education for the next decade quite easily, and fill a multitude of methods texts and journal articles. Such is not the function of this chapter, which is only to put the issues in perspective, to provide an overview of some of the problems in training teachers for today's and tomorrow's schools. Some general areas of our concern can be sketched briefly: these begin with the nature of the young child in the learning situation, his needs and ways of learning, of dealing with information and experience; these factors must provide the starting point to developing better teaching techniques.

Our first recognition is that the young child comes to his first classroom already a complex individual who has been playing and learning for five years. This child has been incorporating the values, the ideas, the strengths, the achievements, the patterns of his particular familial culture. The child is *not* a tabula rasa upon which to place skills which will take root, for she already has ideas and ways of working, thinking, playing; and the teacher, in effect, must clear a growing space in the child's crowded mind for the basic skills and competencies which are necessary for survival in adulthood.

Moreover, it is obvious that the child doesn't have the same experiences as the teacher—they are of different ages, they have different reasons for wanting to learn, they are part of different families and often different cultures. It is the rare teacher who in the process of growing up and 'being schooled' has not lost much of the sense of curiosity, inventiveness, and uninhibited creativity present in the child as she begins school. Even in these earliest years in school, it seems to us to be essential that children see the teacher *not* as the source of the only, or all, truth and the dispenser of unchanging facts and rules, but as an expert learner, a person who continues thinking and exploring and learning with pleasure and who presents information as continuously changing; a person who is open to learn from the child, to share the child's experiences, to listen and to be honest both in her reactions and in talking about the things she doesn't "know" either. To never confess to not knowing something is to tell children that it is possible to know everything, that there is nothing which changes, nothing for an adult to learn, discover, experience which is new—in other words to set oneself up as an impossibly distant perfection, to set unrealistic goals in young minds.

Throughout school, teachers need to emphasize that there is no end to learning and that we need to maintain the "research attitude" to look for new ways of approaching information so that we may extend the boundaries of knowledge. Surely high school students need to meet people who question information and who are able to suggest new ways of looking and to be receptive to the students' occasionally naive outlooks at their field of expertise. Of course the teacher who has made a study of the area has special knowledge—but he or she does not need to present this in such a manner as to suggest that "this is all we know and this is all we need to know."

The teacher must be able to indicate that many scientific ideas came about as a result of playing with concepts and theories and were not simply the inevitable product of a narrow sequence of predictable facts. The scientist daydreams, even nightdreams, and the following up of such ideas has often been exceptionally beneficial to mankind. Similarly, the dramatist treats a universal theme, one present in ancient Greek drama, but does so in the context of his own society, values, and beliefs, and so the conclusion is not necessarily the same—there is no *one* way to believe and feel, even about the same apparent realities. These experiences suggest that having a "mind-full" of information and playing with it, exploring and realigning it is a creative process essential to human evolution on earth; it does *not* suggest that changes in thinking and concepts come about without adequate prior information. We are suggesting that lock-step sequences of learning, and convergent thought as the style of choice in the classroom, create in students' minds the idea that information is static, not to be played with.

Teachers need to be taught to observe more carefully students at work and play, to abstract the child's *own* particular method of organizing reality, to listen to not only *what* the child says but *how* she says it. Much less time could be spent "presenting" material by lecture, film, slides, tapes and books (in effect, less time "on stage"), a necessarily narrow way of collecting feedback in a classroom, and much more time as participant with, or observer-audience for, children working together to access and understand material.

Conversations with students about their ideas and their information, and observations of how they handle and process it, where the child falters and stops understanding, where too much novelty, too much information, has been presented at once and too soon, are critical. By observing, questioning, guiding when necessary, the teacher can see that understanding has been reached; we know by personal experience that often we only understand something when we have verbally articulated it, tossed it around, played with it.

Formal testing is not the only, nor in many cases, the best or most effective, way of assessing understanding of concepts or assimilation of related facts. When understanding comes slowly, more talking and listening, perhaps a new way of explaining the difficult parts, new stimuli or connections for it to understood ideas, may be necessary. Measurement of results of teaching is obtained, with greater difficulty and more time, but also more surely, by watching, listening, looking at the ways in which the student handles the information, evolves ways to explain ideas, connects new ideas to existing knowledge, or applies curiosity and inventiveness to new material.

By all means, teachers are to instruct, to present organized, systematized bodies of fact, knowledge and theory gained in centuries of research and thought, to maximize the child's information about crucial areas, and to provide the student with a wide variety of materials, experiences, and ideas to stimulate creativity—but if the student doesn't absorb all this in one sitting, then the instructional methods, *not* the child, must be questioned and quite possibly altered. The labelling of students as learning disabled, culturally deprived, slow learners or underachievers has become an easy way out, an excuse for not trying alternate methods.

It's about time that society recognized that we, as parents and teachers, approach children in ways that limit their understanding and acquisition of ideas, information, and attitudes as surely as do any innate difficulties within the child. Teachers must be helped to not be afraid to try a different way, to be flexible in the approach to the material (not just to use the handy one-method-only teacher guide that comes with the text), so that all students will have a chance to learn, not just the few who have the inner security to question authority directly. To learn means to take a risk, to stand in a position of saying you don't know, and to begin to look at another way of doing things. If the teacher doesn't do this, how will the student learn to do so?

The major changes required of teachers, then, begin with their attitudes toward themselves as always expert, children as always the ones who must learn. These attitudes imply and lead to certain teaching methods which restrict both teachers and students. We must begin from the other assumption: that every child has experiences, ideas, knowledge—however unsophisticated—to share with all the other people in the classroom, including the teacher, and that it is from a sharing, an understanding, of everyone's pooled knowledge about the world that reality is constructed and altered throughout life. This assumption leads to different, less teacher-centered, more divergent ways of learning about the world.

The teacher training institutions must not only provide access to the most recent information and research results about innovative techniques, methods, and models for teaching, but they must also be able to maintain open-learning situations; encourage dialogues and critical questioning; stimulate inventiveness and divergent thinking; promote a capacity for adaptation and integration of new information into existing conceptual frameworks; explore alternate research models and observational methods for evaluation; and help potential teachers to recognize that changes in society resulting from the advancement of technologies have enormous impact on people, especially children. They must also be able to present new information from the field of developmental psychology in ways which help young teachers to integrate it with their practical experience and personal knowledge. No small task!

Certainly they must continue to "teach" teachers in some of the time honored ways: give demonstrations, provide instructional lectures, distribute information; but just as certainly, they must help the new teacher to develop and maintain the role of a public learner, a planning and perceptive person, a sensitive human knowing when to guide, when to criticize and when not to, when to smile and listen and touch. The teacher so clearly sets the atmosphere, the sense of excitement and exploration as well as the safety to question and sense of belonging, of individual worth, in the classroom, that these emotional components of the art of teaching are too important to be left to chance in the rush to make teaching a science for the 'brave new world'.

The most damning indictments of the failure of teacher training institutions, school systems, school boards, ministries, and teachers to meet the needs of children in contemporary society are not found in editorials about "back to the basics," parents' petitions to school boards, universities' complaints about reading and writing skills of entrants, teachers' unions' complaints about money or lack of it as the root of all failure, businessmen's complaints about lack of appropriate job skills for their particular industry, or unemployment statistics for the unskilled aged 15 to 24. All of these reflect the varied and heavy pressures of a confused society looking for a scapegoat because it seems that the promise that education could solve *all* the world's problems was a fruitless one.

What *is* a damning fact is that so many thousands of students currently in the secondary schools of the industrialized nations—where it is self evident that education and training are critical to personal and economic fulfillment—will probably drop out before graduation, and that most will come from the 30% labelled as "least competent learners." Such students are precisely those who most need preparation for coping with work, parenthood, and the myriad demands of adult life. After decades of curriculum research and revision, the failure of the schools to find ways to involve these students in learning they can see as useful and/or interesting is depressing. What is equally troubling is that economic and political considerations have far more impact on decisions made in education than do ANY of the feelings, needs, and experiences of those most intimately caught up in, and least often consulted by, the system: children and teachers. As long as this is true, hoping for any change in public attitudes, in teacher training and teaching methods, so as to develop a more flexible, responsive, humane educational system, is only a pipedream.

If society can rid itself of its unrealistic expectations for the classroom teacher, and *if* teachers can learn to believe in themselves as teachers again, and *if* teacher training institutions can revamp themselves so that success doesn't just equal the traditional acceptance of some authority's method, and *if* someone decides to consult children of all ages about how they feel about life in classrooms, there is a slight chance that a more flexible method of teaching children to bring their minds and skills to bear on problems in a changing world may evolve.

The key, we think, is to see the teacher's role as an informed guide to help children learn to question before they accept ideas, even 'facts', and to explore all the ways they can of thinking about/learning about/finding out about—by observing people and events, through books, newspapers, films, TV, interviews, by playing; in fact through all their interactions with others and with the environment, through practice, trial and error, experimenting and exploring—in order to master the skills necessary to continually collect feedback in a rapidly expanding world. To learn to process information, to retain what might be most useful, to draw conclusions based on previous knowledge and experience plus new perceptions plus new experiences plus constant thought—this process of treating information maximizes their potential as human beings in evolution.

Most important is the concept that learning isn't something one does in school for a test and then files away under "irrelevant"—it is something one is *open* to every waking moment of one's entire life—a classroom is just one convenient place to meet, to try to organize and structure ideas, to compare them with others' perceptions—those of past and contemporary societies, of one's peers, of authors, of one's teachers and parents—to increase one's understanding of the world and thus make one more able to continue to learn, to bring ideas, facts and skills to bear on new situations and experiences.

This is not a revolutionary new concept for the role of the teacher, or the learner, or the classroom. It is just very hard to reach back to this core philosophy, one Socrates, Rousseau, and Dewey would possibly have espoused, to peel off the system's layers of expectations, social problems, confusion, bureaucracy, power, money and politics, which, like the leaves of an artichoke, form the majority of its bulk. Somewhere within is that for which, as teachers, we instinctively reach—that rare moment when an idea is the spark from one mind to another and excitement flares between them, its light becoming the beacon in the lifelong, awesome, and fascinating search for some understanding of the world, the universe, and ultimately the self. It is, perhaps, our sense that man's only sure immortality is an evolving idea, handed from one generation to another across the centuries. It is what we hold on to, like a drowning person to a passing branch, in the overwhelming and desperate days when being a teacher seems at once too little and too much to achieve.

Chapter 2

THE YOUNG CHILD IN THE CLASSROOM

Most of us accept the idea that we put children into classrooms for at least ten years of their early lives so that they can learn things they need to know to live in this society. Perhaps it is important for those of us who are bound closely to the educational system to stop now and then and re-examine exactly what we are putting children into classrooms *for:* what do we intend them to learn, how does that learning most fruitfully occur, and where and in what ways are we failing? We are most concerned with the experiences of young children in schools, and we would like to examine some of the issues we believe to be most crucial to the education of young children.

We all know that education does not occur in a vacuum; we pay lip service to the idea of beginning where the child is at and taking his individual personality and background into account. But do we *really* recognize the extent to which the young child first entering the school is a product of his own very special world? Let us look at what he brings with him into his first classroom.

First, each child will arrive in that classroom with a bundle of ideas which not only stem from his parents' and his immediate family's attitudes, but also from the feelings, attitudes, and ideas of his neighborhood. He has begun to explore the fields surrounding his house, his backyard, or the gutter at his doorstep, and he has found in these various places many objects and ideas which fascinate him and lead him into further exploration, both physical and mental. Certain objects and materials will be familiar and comfortable to him, and he needs to find these in his classroom too, so that it becomes a *transition* from the home and the neighbourhood into the school.

In the years she has spent at home with her family, the child has formed a picture of herself in relation to other people; as a son or daughter, a brother or sister, niece or nephew or grandchild. She has some ideas about what is appropriate and acceptable to adults who stand in various roles to her, and we can expect it to take some time before the

19

child finds out these things about this new dimension, the classroom and the teacher. If we watch carefully, we find out a good deal about the authority, style, and expectations which are familiar to the child and with which she may initially be most comfortable.

Before discussing further the implications of a child's background and identity for her transition into the school environment, we would like to digress to consider the far more complex problems faced by children who do not speak the primary language of the country in which they live when they enter school; in many of the major industrialized nations such children constitute a sizeable proportion of the student population, both of young children entering kindergartens and of those entering the system as new students throughout elementary and secondary schools. Since we are most familiar with children in the Canadian school system who do not speak English yet, for simplicity's sake, we will refer most often to them, although their experiences can usually be generalized.

It is perhaps impossible for anyone who did not go through it to recognize what a shock school must be at first for such children, whose family patterns or cultural background ill-prepared them for existing in the English-speaking school system. Most of us moved easily to school from homes where we were gradually prepared for school—we learned colours, and numbers, and time concepts, and vocabularies for homes, stores, playgrounds, trips, weather, the seasons—in our family's language. Kindergarten was simply an extension of all those words and the ideas for which they stood. The child whose background has included all these ideas in another language is forced to accommodate himself with great speed and under real pressure to the reality of the "English" classroom. We have seen for years the results of that struggle—for many non-English speaking children, it has equalled failure in school in the early years, especially in learning to read, and has resulted in streaming and perhaps later, in early school leaving.

This is certainly a major problem with which the Canadian schools have as yet failed to deal adequately. A report some time ago to a board of education in Ontario suggested that beginning children's schooling in their first language and gradually introducing English over the first three or four years as the language of instruction might remedy this. A more recent proposal, a bill introduced in the Ontario legislature, would make instruction in a child's first language in academic subjects mandatory in all of Ontario's schools. Obviously this would be nearly impossible to implement in terms of textbooks and teachers, even if it were financially feasible or socially desirable to permanently fragment schools along linguistic and ethnic lines in a society which promotes interdependence and tolerance. Clearly it is necessary for children to learn English, and to have competencies in basic skill areas in English, if they are to function in this society as adults. It would seem to us that the earlier proposal, although also expensive and difficult to implement, makes more sense if children whose first language is not English are to make the transition into an English speaking society with the least possible trauma and waste of human potential.

Quite aside from the academic difficulties experienced by non-English speaking children in their first classrooms and in subsequent years are the psychological implications of such situations. We speak of children coming to school with an identity which is made up largely of their familial patterns and neighbourhood experiences; when that identity is totally denied as important in the child's first exposure to school, where even if the other children speak his language, the teacher and the whole environment are profoundly English-speaking and North American oriented, what is the child to think? Obviously, all that he is, all that his family is, all that he knows, are second rate, and only what he sees in school is acceptable. We are instilling in such children a profound sense of doom, of failure and insufficiency and inferiority, from their very first day in school. Surely this is not what we put children in classrooms for. It is very important, then, that we fully realize in the schools that if the child is to learn well, we must have a thorough understanding of the parental values, the familial environment, the neighbourhood, the language and cultural background, and the child's conception of himself. And we must adapt ourselves, according to what the child already is, inasmuch as that is possible.

The child arriving at school for the first time, then, has a background in her family and community and a cultural identity based on that background; she also knows a lot about learning, since she has been doing so since the moment she could hear and see and feel and taste. She has a clearly developed cognitive, or learning, style, which allows her to look at situations in particular ways, and to approach new ideas or objects in a distinctive manner. This again is largely a product of the ways in which she was encouraged to experience and explore her home environment, and the ways in which adults have structured her world and communicated with her about it.

It is important that the teacher recognize the learning style which the child already has, and then provide him or her with the opportunity to grow from that place, in an environment where he will feel at home and which provides both old and new materials and encourages exploration, curiosity, and questioning. Obviously, the child's adjustment to the school will be greatly enhanced by a teacher who recognizes the child as a real person with a specific personality and learning style rather than as a blank, a name and face to memorize and transform from nonentity into student. This teacher, then, must be a catalyst, a guide, an observer and questioner rather than a demander or an authority.

Every teacher sees daily the wide variance in abilities, skills, learning styles, needs and personality characteristics which is evident even in four or five year olds when they come to school. It is interesting to speculate on the causes for these wide individual variations. Perhaps partly they are a result of heredity; and certainly no behavioural pattern or characteristic can develop without an underlying basis of genetic potentiality. However, it is not really within the scope of this book to discuss heredity and genetic endowment; only to point out that there is always an interaction between the two. In an environment which is beneficial and satisfying to the child, perhaps the genetic endowment blossoms most fully. The less favourable the environment, the less opportunity the genetic capacities of the child have for full development. Thus, a child who has grown up with a severe dietary deficiency will surely show that effect in his later behaviour (Valenzuela, 1989); a child with a very poor diet or one who lacks enough food, for example, often responds either with aggression or feelings of fatigue, and seldom has energy or attention sufficient to allow him to concentrate and learn adequately. Such a child would very probably need to be fed before any learning could actually proceed.

Individual variations in responsivity and sensitivity to the classroom environment and to the teacher are a result not only of general interaction between genotype and environment, but also of the relationship and interaction between parents and child. Not only do the parents influence the child, but the child influences the parents and knows it; and this interaction marches into the classroom with him on the first day. Similarly, not only does the teacher influence the child, but vice versa. Each of us has had a child we had considerable difficulty in working with, one who really turned us off and made us feel guilty as adults and professionals. It is important that we recognize that this is an inevitable part of reactions between two individual human beings and take steps to counter it, because otherwise the child responds to the turn off either by growing aggressive and hostile, or by absenteeism and apathy. Then he is well on the way to failure. The teacher must be aware enough of this kind of individual variation and reaction to try and involve the child positively in classroom activities. It takes a skillful teacher to recognize the effects a child has on her and to try to understand these to the point where her ability to work with the child is not destroyed or negatively influenced.

Sometimes the opposite happens; a teacher is instinctively drawn, occasionally almost obsessively, to a particular child in the classroom, for reasons which are seldom clear. Perhaps the child resembles oneself as a child, or the child one would have liked to be, or a sibling, or one's own child, physically or emotionally, but sometimes it is simply the kind of strong mutual attraction which would be the foundation for a firm friendship between two peers. From the young child's perspective, this may simply be a teacher they admire and like; for the older child it may equal the adoption of the teacher as a role model for their own lives, or, less happily, a painful crush or a severe case of hero worship.

And although the child and teacher may perceive it as enriching their lives, and in fact it may have a very real and long term positive affect on the child's self confidence, there are difficulties inherent in it for both parties and for the other children in the classroom. It may lead to very subjective evaluation of the child's skills and work, and thus make life harder for the child when he or she progresses into the next grade and becomes "ordinary" again; it often makes other children jealous and rejecting of the child and resentful of the teacher, who is no longer seen as "fair." Most of us probably remember the bitterness of watching a "favourite" get all the perks of classroom life pretty vividly. In addition, most of the children who become "the teacher's pet" are those least in need of the extra attention; they tend to be the bright, attractive, articulate middle class kids, not those for whom some extra attention, from anywhere, might make an enormous impact on their starving hearts and minds.

It takes a very honest adult to recognize that very occasionally a child, either liked too much or not enough, will simply be impossible for that adult to work with in a healthy way; such a teacher will not see that as evidence of lack of teaching ability or proof of a personality flaw, but simply as an unfortunate fact which dictates open and frank discussion with the principal about an alternate placement of the child, to be done in such a way that neither the child nor the family sees it as punishment or as a condemnation or rejection of the child as a person. This is obviously a last attempt, a difficult and painful process, but one which is essential to the emotional and psychological well being of both child and teacher.

The child, then, brings many things to school with her: her experiences as part of a family and a community, a cultural identity and language patterns, a distinctive cognitive style, and a wide variance in abilities, skills, and personality characteristics. All of these have contributed to, and make up part of, her self-image, her identity as an individual human being. She has gradually come to perceive herself in ways which say, "I am all right," "I am succeeding," "I am liked"—or the opposites of these attitudes.

The major determinants of a child's self-image seem to be the ways he was provided with stimulation, given adult warmth and comfort, and given gratification and frustration in his family circle. It is our responsibility to understand the particular child-rearing attitudes in a family so that we may add on to these in a meaningful way for the child rather than create distress, distrust, and disillusionment. Children need to have the feeling of love and acceptance and affection and approval from their parents as an ongoing part of their lives. If the learning environment set up in the classroom creates anxiety about these basic needs, then learning cannot proceed effectively. The child's identity is intrinsically bound up with the satisfactions he receives from his home, and teachers must continually be sensitive to this reality.

Just as the child's learning at home has taken place within a close emotional relationship, she is most likely to learn at school when she feels a sense of acceptance and trust from an adult who is sensitive to her, to her ways of learning and communicating and behaving. She will learn best as she has in the earlier years at home—by playing, by doing, by exploring—rather than simply by watching, listening, or memorizing, although these also have their place within the classroom as the child grows older. And she will learn best in her own way and at her own rate, as each of us continues to do with each task or learning situation we approach throughout our lives.

How, then, are we to determine what "in his own way and at his own rate" means for a particular child? It is necessary to have not only information about the individual child's identity and background, but also a clear framework of theoretical information about child development, psychological growth, and what constitutes sound learning experiences for young children. We would like to touch on some of the key issues in these areas, very briefly.

Normal children differ widely in their physical and intellectual development, and it is essential to stress the wide variance in abilities which lies well within the normal range. For example, children show a wide variation in their ability to perform the same act. Some children of four may be able to show fine motor responses in the drawing of a tree, while other children of the same age will only be able to clutch their pencils and make jagged strokes. Some children will be able to understand concepts such as "the house is bigger than a tree," while other children will think that both are big, and bigger than himself, and will be unable to make comparisons. Some children will feel shy, hesitant; others will be vocal, expressive, and spontaneous. Some children will play alongside rather than with their peers, while others will play in a co-operative, involved fashion.

An understanding of child development is vital for the teacher of the young child, as it will permit her to formulate developmental tasks for each child and to base these tasks in relation to the stage of development she has observed in the child. If the child is successful at a particular task, he is encouraged by his success to move on to tackle new achievements; failure leads only to frustration and unhappiness, and is an unnecessary factor in the primary classroom. Therefore it is up to the teacher to set the stage for learning by observing the developmental capacities of her children, and encouraging them, by altering the environment through the addition of new material or through her questions, to explore further or try a different task.

The varied experiences which are provided for children in the classroom will encourage intellectual questioning and growth. Several theories of intellectual development have been elaborated during the past years; theorists like Hebb, Hull, Skinner, Mazlow, Tolman, and Piaget have presented various views of how intelligence develops and learning takes place. There is not, at this point, a comprehensive theory of human learning, but the various people who have worked in this field have contributed much to our understanding of intellectual process. Perhaps one of the most important things that comes through in most of these learning theories is that a child's active doing and involving herself in her learning environment is a necessary condition for intellectual stimulation and growth and subsequent comprehension and acquisition of competencies.

Of all these people, perhaps Piaget (1952) has provided us with the most considerable understanding of the learning process, and he certainly stresses that action is important, perhaps even vital, in learning. Intelligence and mental development are a spiralling progression, with the child's doing and acting forming the base of each spiral. Each act seems to be repeated, with an increasingly varied and wider number of acts being joined together to form more complex ways of acting, more ways of playing. The co-ordination of these acts permits greater experimentation for the child, and thereby greater learning.

Piaget describes the various steps through which the child moves in achieving intellectual growth, pointing out that the child goes through these stages at various rates, and that children differ in the ages at which they reach each stage. Piaget felt, however, that all children go through all stages in about the same kind of sequential fashion. He felt that the child had to acquire and maintain the functioning involved at each stage, for it provided the basis for the next stage. These stages include the sensory-motor stage, the pre-operational stage, the concrete operational stage, and the formal operations stage.

Piaget has contributed much to our understanding of the child's early intellectual growth and development, but his insistence on stage dependent sequential development for all children is one which we cannot really share because it leaves so little room for individual variation, and does not help us to understand that sometimes children move back and forth in rather random ways, jumping or bypassing "special stages."

As well as plentiful factual information about intellectual development, teachers need a thorough understanding of the complexities of the dependency relationships between young children and their parents, most generally their mothers, if they are to cushion the child's initial adjustment to school and facilitate sound continued psychological growth. The attitude of the mother to the child seems to be the most important and vital factor in the child's emotional development, and there are many research studies leading us to recognize that this interactive influence upon the child has subsequent effects upon his physical development, his intellectual achievement, and his psychological growth.

For example, very early continued separation of the mother from the infant seems to result in the "wasting away" of the child, physically and psychologically. Early rejection of the child seems to result in an overly independent and, at times, anti-social child. Overprotectiveness seems to result in an anxious child who wants to please and is fearful of expressing any kind of aggression (Weininger, 1986). That these attitudes have an effect on learning is well documented, and children who have been reared in such atmospheres seem to be the children who are destined to require special help.

Where the child is not provided with sufficient individual stimulation and encouragement, either because there is a weak attachment between mother and infant, or because the familial atmosphere is such that the child is not encouraged to explore, to learn, to talk with his mother, to play, then the child is deprived, and will, no doubt, require greater encouragement in the classroom in order to be able to learn successfully.

It is important for teachers to recognize that dependency relationships are the kind with which young children feel safest, with which they are most familiar. A certain amount of transference of the child's relationship with her mother to her first teacher is thus almost inevitable; not only does the child know best how to relate in that way, but it fills her needs for continuity, security, and predictability until she finds her feet in this new environment. Thus it is very important for the classroom teacher to be the kind of person who feels okay about touching and comforting and holding children, about providing warmth and lots of care.

This is true not only in the lower grades, but all the way through the high school years; the one way to guarantee safety and acceptance to children of all ages is by our willingness to extend ourselves physically as well as verbally to them. Children know something we often forget: it is quite possible to lie to someone in words, almost impossible to do so with touch. Mutual respect and trust are expressed by the gentle, non-threatening and non-sexual touch of one person to another, and our schools would be the richer if we could remember that it is trust which underlies our learning experiences from the day we take our first step, secure in the knowledge that mother is there to catch us if we fall.

Another basic part of the dependency relationship of child to mother, child to teacher, is the need for unconditional acceptance. A child needs to know, for sure and for always, that even if you as an adult reject his behaviour in no uncertain terms, you accept him as a person—he is not dumb or stupid or crazy or careless or lazy in your eyes, either through your words or your actions, just because a particular piece of behaviour is one of these things. Every action, every word, every touch needs to transmit the feeling to the child that, "Even if I do not like what you just did, and I will not allow you to do it again, I like *you.* You are NOT your behaviour—it is only a part of your way of dealing with people which you can alter and change."

Thus trust and acceptance of the child as a valuable person, coupled with the ability to let the child determine what his own needs for dependence and independence are at a given time, are the basis for a viable and satisfying relationship between child and teacher. The teacher is not in competition with the child's mother or family, but rather a continuation of the security which they provide, a bridge to a scary but exciting world. The child needs to be able to maintain a relatedness to his family and his environment, and the teacher must recognize this need, and not alienate a child from his family, rather to help integrate the new classroom experiences in such a way that he participates rather than withdraws, feels safe and comfortable rather than left out and scared, and has a sense of joy, of fulfillment and promise, rather than a sense of doom and alienation. The child should be able to move between home and school equally comfortably, with his own sufficiency and belongingness in both places.

Possibly the most heartbreaking times in a teacher's life are when a child is clearly at risk, emotionally or physically, in the home, and comes into the classroom withdrawn, scared, lonely, alienated, untrusting, and in deep need of caring and acceptance that are evidently missing at home. Often if a teacher can penetrate the defensive wall the child has created to protect a very fragile being, she is then the recipient of all the caring and needing feelings the neglected child has not had filled for so long. This can be a very overwhelming feeling for the teacher, especially since there is the clear knowledge that one cannot "fix" what is wrong at home and guarantee the child the love and acceptance which is every child's birthright.

The temptation is always there to back off, to disclaim responsibility in the face of the needs of all the other kids or one's own family. Another reality in such a situation is that almost inevitably the teacher resents or dislikes the parents she has never seen, and the feeling is likely to be mutual, because even parents who "don't seem to care" usually do, and often feel terribly guilty about their inability to nurture the child, and thus resentful of someone who is able to give their child what they cannot. But with the help of the school psychologist, social worker, or guidance counsellor, the classroom teacher CAN help such a child by providing an oasis of warmth in his bleak world.

Assuring the emotional and psychological growth of twenty-eight or so bodies is sometimes a seemingly impossible job, especially for the young teacher faced with a lot of theories, differing expectations about what should be taught or learned and when and how. How does one begin to translate all kinds of theories and children's needs into sound learning experiences and a nourishing classroom environment? For generations, teachers have said, "For heaven's sake, no more theories! Tell me what I can DO to help kids learn best!"

We believe that helping kids learn is best done through the medium of early childhood play. Play *is* the child's way of learning — it is the work of early childhood, neither as simple nor as pointless as most adults have come to believe. It is through the process of exploring, bumbling about, creating a mess and arriving at the other end smiling in satisfaction that a child gets the feeling of being able to accomplish and achieve, which is the feeling we want to encourage and promote in the schools. It is through play that the child gains the satisfactions she needs to allow her to continue to learn, later, other kinds of things which we too frequently mistakenly believe are the sole subject matter suitable to schools.

Play does a lot of things for kids. First, it's fun — and that is important. If you watch young children play, though, you soon recognize that it is also serious business for them — it is the child's way to explore herself and the world around her and her relationships to it without prematurely coming to any conclusions. Premature decision making and rote learning result in inadequate learning because the process, the working through, has been by-passed or short circuited. Everyone has seen the young child who can count to twenty by the age of three without the slightest conceptual understanding of what a number is or how it represents objects or groups of objects and as such can be manipulated. That knowledge comes only through play, not memorization.

Play allows the child to experiment with unresolved situations or problems he perceives around him, and to solve these for himself. The child who doesn't understand why water doesn't pour up, gradually explores not only the concepts involved in water play, like volume, but also the abstract concept of up and down. The child begins to relate "liquid-down" and "gravity-pull" and a host of other concepts in his play, and thus in his exploration of why water doesn't pour up, he finds out many other things about the physical properties of water and gravity.

Play facilitates the cognitive growth of the child by permitting him and encouraging him to *do*, rather than being *done to* or being *told* what to do. It is a learning process consisting of sequences involved in creative patterns like changing, designing, questioning, combining, organizing, integrating, simplifying. It involves judgemental patterns for the child, like defining, choosing, contrasting, comparing, criticizing, and evaluating. It involves discriminating patterns such as collecting, re-organizing, classifying, matching, ordering, describing, explaining, communicating, identifying, and listening, and many others. As the child goes through these patterns in play, he learns to be attentive and to listen, to perceive and to understand, to try and to interpret and then to communicate. Along with this, he remembers what he has done, because for him, this behaviour has been meaningful, not simply imposed on him by adults.

So what we believe teachers need most to do in classrooms with young children is let them play—and watch, and listen, and smile, and touch, and be aware of the times when the child is ready to move on, to have new materials added to his environment, to explore in different ways, to communicate his frustration or joy or questions or fears, to ask questions—and to respond to all these needs with common sense and kindness. The teacher who is aware of all those things which a child brings to school, and who brings all these things to school herself, is able to provide a curriculum focusing on environmental change in the classroom through encouragement of individual variations and needs. She understands the child's developmental capacities, paces and adjusts the learning situations for him and with him, is aware of his needs for success and achievement, dependence and independence, and builds with each of her children the close positive emotional relationship which is the foundation of all meaningful human experiences.

We are often painfully aware of when we are failing as educators, or as part of a system—but how do we know when we're succeeding? If the children in your classroom get up most mornings eager to come to school, excited and happy to share another day with each other and you, and if you come to school each day glad to be there, excited about and challenged by what happens between you and the children in your room, in spite of the long days and the hard times, then you *know* why it is good for them to be there, what schools are really for, what teaching can really be—and there isn't much we can tell you about the young child in the classroom that you don't already know!

It is like being a parent—there are always lots of experts to tell you what to do and what not to do, but in the final analysis it is what you FEEL about what you DO with children that counts. And teachers, like parents, often know more than they think they know. If you feel good about what goes on in your classroom, chances are that the children do too; and chances are that they are learning the important things about being people living and working with, sharing and caring about, other people. All other learning, academic skills and competencies are built upon this foundation; without it, there IS no point in putting children, or teachers, in classrooms.

Chapter 3

WHAT DO THE PROBLEMS OF CLASS SIZE AND ACID RAIN HAVE IN COMMON?

On the simplest possible level, it is self-evident that the more children one has to care for, the less time is available for each individual; the mother trying to cope with four preschool children at once, the camp counsellor keeping an eye on ten active eight-year-olds outdoors, the kindergarten teacher trying to get 28 children in and out of the bathroom and into winter clothing for recess, the primary teacher attempting to listen to one reading group while monitoring the behaviour and study of four other groups doing seatwork, the teacher of intermediate students in a class of 38 trying to find time to work carefully with each one on their writing and still teach the class as a whole, the secondary English teacher who has taught the same curriculum to classes of 32 and 20, and found her marking load decrease significantly—each of these can, from this personal experience, tell us that smaller numbers mean more attention for each child in their care.

And yet the issue is more complex than this. Many factors combine to create a learning environment: the age, capabilities, and aptitudes of the students, their emotional readiness for learning, their interpersonal skills, their sociometric backgrounds, the objectives of the course or unit and of a particular lesson, the methodology used by the teacher, the availability of effective teaching materials, the empathy of the teacher and her overall competence, to list only the most major ones.

Certainly class size is an important factor, but it is intertwined with other factors in a way which makes isolating it for research purposes very difficult, as is often the case in doing educational research on any single variable. For example, a class of ten might be too large if the children range in age from five to twelve, have diverse emotional and educational needs and levels of functioning, and are being taught by an untrained teacher unfamiliar with their social and economic background, in an ill-equipped space with insufficient materials of relevance to the children.

33

This is not as unlikely as it seems: many of the one room schoolhouses we have endowed with such fond memories could be described accurately in such a manner, as could some of today's isolated schools in the sparsely populated rural area of many countries.

In addition, we need to carefully define the term "class size" itself: it must certainly be considered in terms of a desired outcome, not as if it exists in isolation. Unfortunately, too often newspaper reports of negotiations between teachers' organizations and school boards tend to wave the flag of "Class Size" without defining such desired outcomes or goals. If well-regimented classes are the goal, class size is probably not the most important issue: teachers with a firm sense of control recognize little difference between keeping 20 or 30 or 40 students quiet. For rote learning of grammar/spelling/math/history facts, class size is irrelevant; many experienced teachers have taught kids coming from other countries where class sizes are in excess of 60 and students are able to recite these facts impressively, even if they are not necessarily able to apply them. If the methodology is films and lectures, most adults who experienced university classes in the hundreds can see no relevance in a discussion of class size. The kinds of learning which can easily be evaluated by standardized academic skills testing may be more affected by the variables of teachers "teaching to the test" and the individual motivation of students to achieve for themselves or their parents, than by class size per se.

The question, as we see it, is not whether young children can be controlled in large groups, nor whether the majority of them can make sufficient academic progress in such classes. Our main concern with class size is how we can meet young children's affective and physical needs most effectively, as it is our strong belief that these needs must be met before children are able to cope with cognitive learning.

We have known for a long time that early childhood is a critical period for the establishment of a self-concept, dependency relationships, curiosity, imagination, trust, and a host of other characteristics and approaches to living which make later academic progress more likely and more satisfying for an individual child. As *Education in the Primary and Junior Divisions*, the Ontario Ministry of Education's 1975 guideline, puts it, "The child's sense of self-identity is another key influence on learning processes. Knowing oneself and finding worthiness in that self are basic human needs. To respond to these needs, the teacher must care for the children and be sensitive to each individual child's progress. Teachers *must* show that they care. Children need to have these basic needs for security and self-esteem satisfied before they can begin to attend to learning in school."

This philosophy is very humane and child-centered, and certainly not one which any parents, teachers, administrators or trustees would take issue. The problem is determining the degree to which small class size contributes positively to making such a philosophy operative in the schools, and thus to achieving the characteristics we see as most desirable for human development and for later academic learning. Complicating this problem are two external but extremely important groups of factors: family and social change, and economic and political priorities.

This chapter sets out to summarize very briefly the relevant research on class size and affective needs, to consider the impact of family and social change on the structure of schooling, and to suggest some of the economic and political issues which affect the funding of schools and the size of classes.

For the purposes of this paper the definitions for "small" class size are taken from *To Herald a Child* (La Pierre, 1978). In it, LaPierre writes, "It is my view that class size does affect a child's development and in many instances it may well be crucial. I have been told that I should aim at suggesting the "bearable maximum." This could be: junior kindergarten, 15; senior kindergarten, 20; Grade 1, 22; Grades 2 and 3, 25. However, it would be presumptuous on my part to agree with this proposal. Furthermore, when involved in the life of a child, the "bearable maximum" cannot be contemplated." (p. 28). In his conclusion, LaPierre recommends for his proposed centres an overall ration of adult to child of 1:6, with teachers responsible for no more than 12 children at a time, and coordinating teachers for no more than 20. It should, of course, be recognized that since classes this small virtually do not exist in the primary years except in exceptional cases, there is little research information which substantiates these as most desirable—they are very much an ideal number arrived at after looking at the difficulties inherent in much larger classes (Tizard, 1974).

Those difficulties are described quite accurately by Hart (1981): "The classroom grouping is the wrong size for all activities except rote—too small for films, lectures and visitors; too large for discussions, projects, field trips and the like. . . . In reading, one child may bring 3,000 hours of experience with books to the beginning classroom, a second child 300 hours, a third none worth mentioning. There is simply no way a teacher can deal with these differences. Only one to one tutoring will possibly work. : ... Disciplinary remarks and actions may take more time than instruction ... in actuality, almost none of the "individualization" that gets talked about happens: simply putting a child into a different group may be called individualizing ... little time is given to actual instruction in classrooms. Management, busywork, waiting, leaving and arriving, and other diversions reduce gross instructional time to around ninety minutes a day.... In-class attention to single students may average, per student, only six hours per year" (p. 10–11).

Some studies have indicated that the major difference a smaller class size makes is in the perception of the teacher. Wright's 1977 study concluded that "the teachers expected the two smaller classes (16 and 23) to be different from the large classes (30 and 37), especially in the amount of individuation possible. Their experience with the smaller classes as they perceived it supported this expectation. Even though the observationist data did not seem to give these findings much support, they must not be ignored. It does make a positive difference to the teacher to work in a smaller class" (p. 118). However, he also noted that "the attitudes toward school are unlikely to change and the teachers' instructional style will not likely change either" (p. 125). And as far as academic achievement is concerned, "a statistically significant plan size effect in mathematics concepts was found. There were no significant differences found in the measures of reading, vocabulary or mathematics, problem solving, measures of the students' development in art and composition based on samples of the students' work showed no differences between changes." (p. 123)

Shapiro (1975) concentrated on four-year-olds in a study which looked at child-teacher contacts, either alone or in a group. The contacts increased as the pupil-teacher ratio decreased until there were two teachers for 16 pupils. She found that total class size was important as well, since if there were more than 20 students in a class the number of child-teacher contacts did not increase when additional teachers were added. From this she concluded: "It seems that the presence of more adults did not outweigh the disadvantages to the child of always being part of a crowd."

Another widely quoted study is Cannon's early research (conducted in 1955, reported in 1966) of two groups. Although her sample was small, her findings are interesting and indicative of certain characteristics of small and large classes. Furthermore, her "small" was quite large by research standards, averaging 24.8 children, while the "large" had an average of 38.5 students. These are probably, however, quite realistic numbers in terms of teachers' perceptions of "small" and "large," if we base them on reality, not research!

She observed that there were more aggressive acts in the larger group; considerable waiting for the use of equipment, and a longer time between turns at a favourite activity. Also, the teacher had fewer opportunities to guide children individually in order to minimize negative actions. The smaller group appeared to achieve more fully integrated group relationships, and the teacher became a more significant person in the life of the child. The climate of the small class seemed to foster more creative, dramatic, and social experience in these activities. In the larger group there was more noise, greater excitement, and an atmosphere less conducive to cooperative, creative play. The teacher obtained more satisfaction, more enjoyment and a higher sense of achievement when working with the smaller group. Although these results seem very positive, it should be remembered that this study was done over 30 years ago, when both kids and teachers had different expectations for classroom behavior and activities, and is very subjective, and thus more difficult to measure in terms of the categories used, like "fully integrated group relationships," "social experience," "atmosphere less conducive to co-operative, creative play" and "higher sense of achievement."

Cohen's research in 1966 centered on dependency needs in young children and the relationship between three types of dependencies and class size. He outlined these as:

- emotional-social dependency: children need supportive caring and love from a caregiver, as well as to being able to trust and depend on adults. He raises the question of how many equally needy (as all young children basically are) students can successfully share one teacher.
- cognitive-intellectual dependency: as a student grows older and gains more skill and knowledge, he is able to move away from the person who presents the material to the material itself. Cohen maintains that a too large class size may increase rather than decrease dependency, as a teacher is unable to guide and supervise the early efforts at independence when there are too many children.
- concrete/sensory dependency: the young child needs to explore the immediate world around him or her by actually doing. It is important to consider under what circumstances children will be able to do this.

Porwell (1978) summarized much of the research literature up to that date, and drew some tentative conclusions, none of which are really surprising, given our understanding of the complexity of the relationships between various components of classroom life. His major findings can be summarized in the following manner:

- the relationship between pupil achievement and class size is highly complex.
- small classes seem to be important to increased pupil achievement in reading and math in the early primary grades.
- there is some evidence of a positive relationship between small class size and pupil achievement when primary grade pupils are taught in small classes for two or more consecutive years.
- pupils with lower academic ability tend to benefit more from smaller classes than do pupils with average ability.
- smaller classes may positively affect the academic achievement of economically or socially disadvantaged students.
- methods and quality of instruction, rather than the number of students, need to be considered in measurements of classroom effectiveness.
- more individualization, creativity, group activity, and respect for the needs of others seem to occur more frequently in smaller than larger classes, but not enough research has been done to validate the presumed superiority of these activities in terms of student academic achievement.

In summary, there is not adequate research to support the contention that class size is the single or most important determinant of academic achievement. However, larger classes do seem to make it very easy for an individual child to be lost in the crowd. They make artificial formality and structure more necessary, and children are more likely to be dealt with only as part of a mass. They are likely to discourage the individual attention necessary for social and emotional growth. Young children need time to explore, manipulate, play and socialize, as well as time alone to reflect, and time for a one-to-one relationship with the "significant other" who is their nursery or primary teacher, just as they need these in their lives at home with a parent or caregiver.

Given that more and more children are in institutionalized settings from the preschool years in our society, it should be our goal to make these as home-like as possible, with caring adults who have time for each child in a warm environment. Both research and our own intuition as teachers and parents support the idea that in early childhood "education" and "caring" are, or should be, synonymous, and large classes are not as likely to foster this condition for children.

There has always, of course, been a strong connection between social change and resulting changes in education; one need only consider the impact of changes in child labour laws during the Industrial Revolution on the structure and duration of public education, for example. And reformers have always been conscious of the impact of education in return on society; Dewey's question, of whether the schools exist to perpetuate the existing social order or to teach children to question/change, it is perennially relevant. So it should come as no surprise that the changes in the structure of the family, particularly in the last two decades, have brought about the need for adaptation within the school system. A recent study by Ronald Burke of York University (March, 1984), "Economic Recession and the Quality of Education: Some Threatening Trends," describes how severely major changes in Canadian society are impacting on public education.

About 10% of children in Canadian schools today are currently from single parent families, and an additional number live in "blended" families; this seems not to be a significant number until it is equated with real bodies in classrooms. In an average primary classroom, this may be anywhere from 3–7 children! In addition, the tensions of hard times economically, and the resulting unemployment and stress within the family unit, expose more children to higher than normal levels of anger (and possibly aggression) within the family. For such children school is often their only refuge from unhappiness, and the presence of an adult to provide a listening ear and a shoulder to cry on, as well as a positive, supportive role model, is essential.

Success at school and within the peer culture becomes doubly necessary for children whose stability at home is threatened, but often their ability to achieve these two things is eroded substantially by their preoccupation with what is happening at home. They can't pay attention in class, or focus at home on homework, and thus their relationships with teachers and their marks suffer. They are often withdrawn, depressed, or irritable with friends, which may lead to their peer group leaving them out because it's no fun to be with someone who is always down. It is essential that classroom teachers have the time and energy to pick up on such behaviors, either to counsel the child themselves or to urge the student to seek help from guidance counsellors. Thus the tasks of the teacher have expanded beyond the traditional academic and interpersonal functions in trying to deal with the affective needs of children caught in family and economic crises. Often the time needed for individual support of children in such situations is next to impossible to find, particularly when the class is large.

Another by-product of economic pressure is the increasing numbers of children from homes where both parents work. For young children, this often means institutionalized or non-family daycare at an early age; for school age children this may equal nine hours or more spent at school, in before-school, lunchtime, and after-school programs of one variety or another. Schools seldom have either the facilities or the personnel to provide quality programming of this sort; most generally it is just a room where there is minimal adult supervision and low-level organization of relatively quiet games and indoor activities.

For those who go home after school to an empty house, or to older brothers' and sisters' care, television is often the only substitute for human communication. In most neighborhoods, stay-at-home mothers are deluged, if they seem at all willing, with their children's friends looking for human contact, warmth, a snack, a place to feel safe. Even at the intermediate and secondary level, the increase in the numbers of kids who "just hang around" the halls or locker banks or nearby malls, or who seek out a teacher "just to be with" after school has increased. By this age most of them are quite openly verbal about "not going home because there's no one there anyway and it's lonely with just the TV, so I might as well stay here/go someplace with my friends." One wonders how many kids take on after school jobs to provide not only money, but people to be with and a structure, a place to feel needed by others.

Panzica (1983), a senior consultant to Ontario's Council on Drug Abuse, notes that many parents are not currently fulfilling their traditional roles: " . . . indicators of parental abdication include wanting the school to teach the child a love of books, as well as how to read; wanting the church to teach morals unaided; insisting that someone else teach life skills. One of the saddest things of the last 30 years is the decline in parental teaching, especially teaching by fathers." (p. 58) Experienced teachers have also noted with dismay the expectation that the schools provide virtually all cultural exposure—trips to concerts, plays, museums and historical sites are now frequently organized by the school to fill the family vacuum, as are camping trips, sports, and outdoor education of all sorts.

By and large, the school system has not found effective ways to cope with these changes in the family. As it is unrealistic to assume society will ever go back to the way it was, schools, like it or not, seem on the way to becoming comprehensive social agencies, with the responsibility for values and sex education, vision, hearing, and dental care, arts appreciation and outdoor skills, life skills training, socialization, recreation and fitness, counselling, job training and placement: all the myriad tasks once performed, more or less consciously, by nuclear and extended families and the community at large. If this is to be the case, there seem to be only two alternatives: cut class size drastically and choose and train teachers who can function as surrogate parents as well as counsellors and recreation specialists, or be prepared to hire additional staff who will take on these responsibilities for the half of the day children are increasingly IN school but NOT in an academic setting.

There is also an increased awareness, courtesy largely of the media, of the other social byproducts of changes within the society: increases in child suicide and depression, alcoholism and drug abuse, violent crime and vandalism, sexual assaults, physical and sexual abuse, youth gangs, AIDS, prostitution, and so forth. Concern about coping with these as they impact on children in schools is growing, although fortunately most non-inner city primary school children still seem insulated from many of these, at least in terms of personal experience. "Street proofing" children, as well as presentations to help victims of physical or sexual abuse, are appearing with some regularity in the schools. Whether the schools possess the capacity, either in terms of personnel or finances, to counter such severe psychological/sociological hazards, either in terms of prevention or treatment, seems doubtful to us. Indications are that society's expectations for what the school can and should achieve are unrealistic, especially given current funding levels and increasing shortages of teachers in many areas.

But if the raising and socialization of young children is to be left almost wholly to the educational system, while fewer financial and human resources are to be available for this most important human objective, where do we turn?

Although there seems to be little to be gained by trying to make parents feel guilty—after all, they are not responsible for the changing nature of the society any more than schools are—some far-reaching discussion on the roles of parents, schools, and society in the socialization and education of children is definitely needed. We need to stop looking for who to blame for this mess (the traditional posture of schools vs. parents vs. trustees vs. theoreticians vs. governments) and start looking for ways to improve it—together! Only through such parent mobilization, we suspect, will the political pressure necessary to effect changes in the school's capacity to deal with family and social change emerge.

One has only to note the extremely successful pressure brought to bear for French Immersion schooling in Ontario: once convinced of the educational/social usefulness it promised for their children, parents' pressure groups have been quite successful in enlarging a very expensive program, even in a time of great fiscal restraint in education. Any movement toward decreasing class size in order to better meet children's affective needs and to increase the capacity of the schools to cope with social problems becomes, ultimately, a political task as much as an educational one. No matter how much research evidence in favour of smaller primary classes might be generated, and how many primary teachers can give witness to its direct relevance to the life of their classrooms, and how many experts extol the virtue of adults spending more time with individual children in a troubled society, it is only political pressure which will achieve these changes.

Unfortunately, society is not prepared to believe that teachers have unselfish motives when they speak out for smaller class sizes. Public opinion tends to the position that teachers are already overpaid for their short hours and ten-month year, and that demands for smaller classes are just another way to cut their work load. This view is too often shared by trustees, who certainly ought to know better!

A 1976 article from MAST, the official publication of the Manitoba Association of School Trustees, stated: "While reductions in class size can often be justified in terms of teachers' sanity, pleasant classroom atmosphere and other advantages, they are hard to justify in terms of test scores. . . . Children do not automatically learn more because they are in smaller classes. In fact, achievement in smaller groups is not always as great because the spirit of competition, interaction and the opportunity to learn from others are not as prevalent . . . Larger classes make group competition as well as individual competition possible. Also, smaller classes may limit the opportunity for students to learn how to work together and some projects may not be possible . . . lowering class size does not automatically guarantee a change in teaching methods. . . . MAST president, Ken Burgess, states "school boards are not prepared to decrease class size until they are satisfied that the quality of education will improve with smaller classes. . . . Trustees obviously want the best quality of education for their students but believe that all factors which contribute to quality education need to be examined before more dollars are plunged into the coffers." (p. 26, 27)

While certainly all factors do need to be considered, this emphasis on the importance of teaching competition as opposed to co-operation seems distinctly at odds with what we know of the affective needs of young children, not to mention the larger needs of the society itself. In fact, there is very little recognition in this article of the school's need to base structure and content on the affective needs and learning styles of children. We find it interesting, too, that the assumption is made that teacher sanity is not very important to the life of the classroom!

In the "Report on Declining Enrolment in Ontario," commissioned by the Ministry of Education, Jackson (1978) makes a recommendation that class size should be reduced so that the goal of individualized instruction can be realized. In "Issues and Directions," the Ministry's response (1980), the problem of reducing class size is addressed to the teacher federations as an issue to be negotiated in collective bargaining. One could infer from this that class size is not considered a priority by the government. In recent Ontario elections, many campaign promises were made about reducing class size in the primary years, and specific numbers were outlined as a goal during that government's early days in office. But in the face of a decreasing slice of the provincial budget allotted to education, and in light of the impending teacher shortage, it would seem unlikely that such reductions in class size will ensue unless such a policy is seen as having widespread and vocal public support.

This conflict between announced policy and the provision of funds to implement it is, however, in line with other government policies on education in the last few years; Ontario's Bill 82 (on the provision of integrated special education for all kinds of disabilities within every school system) requires vast financial support, for example, as does the province of Ontario's decision in 1986 to fund the separate (Roman Catholic) school system through public funds. Building new schools and renovating the increasing number of older, crumbling buildings will also be expensive as population shifts continue to occur, and funding for an increasing number of English as a Second Language classes in the larger urban boards will be expensive. Provision of updated facilities in the universities, especially for primary research in the sciences, and of computer facilities at all levels of education is essential. The level at which the cost of a university education becomes inaccessible to all but the upper middle class is rapidly approaching, if it is not already here. Yet the province's contribution to educational funding at all levels has been a constantly decreasing percentage over the last decade. Close examination of the situation in other Canadian provinces and across the

United States, Britain, and Europe would, we expect, reveal similar sad realities.

Obviously, governments see education as less of a priority than it was when a more substantial percentage of the population was of school age, and unfortunately there are many citizens who do not see why education should be funded at all by those who do not have children, or whose children are grown. This is analogous, of course, to the idea that hospitals be funded only by those who are sick, roads by those who use cars, and so forth; it is a very short sighted view to take, since education benefits an entire society. *Wise* investment in education should decrease the amounts which must later be spent on remediating social problems and retraining adults for a changing work world; how to achieve such *wise* investment is, of course, one of the major concerns for all educators and politicians alike!

To summarize:

1. education and caring cannot be separated when referring to young children.
2. young children require fairly small grouping in home-like settings due to the nature of their emotional, social, cognitive and physical development.
3. there is a great need for parent education and involvement in the education of children, both at home and through the schools.
4. changes within the family and the society necessitate changes in the schools to help children, their families, and the society at large.
5. political pressure for careful analysis of funding priorities and methods is necessary to achieve educational goals and to effect needed changes.

We feel that we cannot afford to compromise with the lives of young children; to do so has far reaching consequences for the future of society as a whole. It is time we persuaded politicians and governments that the education of children is a priority of all of us, requiring long-term planning and preventive strategies rather than short term compromises and remediational tactics after the damage is done. Class size is but one issue, one factor in the creation of a quality educational system, but we feel it is a key issue if we are to actually do what we say we intend to do " . . . to nurture every child's growth so that each may be able to continue his or her education with satisfaction and may share in the life of the community with competence, integrity, and joy." *The Formative Years, 1975*

So we suggest that, humour aside, it *is* kind of like the acid rain problem—we *know* a certain percentage of acid rain is caused by a handful of coal/sulphur emitting sources in major industrial societies, and that cleaning them up *now* will prevent more damage to lakes and forests. But *if* we wait another twenty years for the *definitive* study to discover all the sources and work out the best, most complex technological solution possible, we will have irretrievably lost vast tracts of North America and Northern Europe to acid rain damage in the meantime.

Likewise, we *know* smaller class sizes, particularly in the pre-school, kindergarten, and early primary years, will help a large number of children to grow and learn better if implemented *now*. But *if* we wait another twenty years for the *definitive* study, and then for the development of other, more complicated strategies to deal with social change, parent involvement, and political and economic prioritizing, we will have denied vast numbers of the children of this world their chance to bloom.

The answer, then, to the question of the title, "What do the problems of class size and acid rain have in common?" is, "They both require our attention NOW!!"

Chapter 4

EDUCATING THE CHILD
FOR THE 21ST CENTURY

"*H*ow *is a rabbit?*" might seem like a strange question to you, and perhaps you would reply, *"Certainly you mean what is a rabbit?!"* Much of education has been concerned with *what* a rabbit is. We think education should try instead to provide children with opportunities to experience the "howness" of a rabbit: how does it move, wiggle its tail, eat, shake its legs, twitch its nose, clean itself, communicate with its young, build its nest, and so forth.

Learning has traditionally been seen as the acquisition of *facts* and *skills* imparted by a succession of resources: books, films, and teachers, for the most part; and certainly these kinds of information and sources continue to be important today. But for children who will be adults in the 21st century, in a rapidly changing and technologically dominated world, this is surely a too-restrictive definition. If we think of learning as the acquisition of *ideas* and *skills* through experience, as a way of providing knowledge which helps to clarify thinking and sharpen images in a child's mind, then the provision of open-ended experiences is essential to the process.

Too often educators are intent on imparting a framework within which they expect a child to operate, forcing a child to learn what questions to ask when, rather than helping him explore the way in which something operates or helping him deal with everyday realities in an open, natural fashion. The tendency is to provide a total concept for a child before he has a chance to explore the ideas around it sufficiently. This leads to premature concept formation, limited understanding, and rigid or circumscribed conceptualization, often preventing further exploration or expansion in the face of increasing knowledge. We must begin to seriously question whether we want to lock children into an educational system which discourages connections with everyday realities and limits the possibilities for creativity and curiosity.

47

One of the first activities the very young child undertakes is sensory exploration; it is vital to the development of understanding and thus to all learning and education. Too often adults use words, which are only symbols, instead of objects with very young children. But it is only when a child can associate meaning with an object that the word for the subject makes any sense to him. For example, if you were to ask a child to "mount the ladder", you would probably get a blank stare, whereas if you were to ask him to *climb* the same ladder he would probably know what you mean, because most little children have been told "Don't climb on that or you'll fall down and hurt yourself"—followed by a fall. Only through concrete experience does a child fill an empty word with the images which make that word of symbolic value to him.

Even a two-dimensional image, such as a picture in a book or on television, is not an adequate substitute for sensory exploration of the concrete object. A young child may learn the names for "truck" and "bus" and "car" from a picture book and still not recognize which is which on the highway, because the sizes are not predictable from the picture in a book, and he may not realize that colour or specific design is not necessarily a part of the definition of the word or the object, as it is a part of the picture. Thus learning in a didactic fashion is often a pointless and empty exercise for the young child.

The concept of sensory exploration as related to the acquisition of knowledge seems easy enough to understand. However, there are practical problems involved; many people misunderstand, or cannot accept, that this is "really learning." It is not straightforward information-receiving or collecting of subject matter. Many parents insist that children acquire what they accept as a state of knowledge, rather than ways of knowing. Lillian Katz (1969), in a speech at a conference on the education of young children some years ago, put it very well:

"Today large numbers of preschool teachers are actively involved in trying to help parents to see the soundness of their views, methods, techniques, styles and goals for young children. Many teachers . . . have a sophisticated and complex view of the nature of learning and development. They talk of children's learning through play, through sensory motor experiences, through peer group activities, through self-selected activities, creative activities, exploration, and experimentation. They make complex assumptions about the psychodynamics of growth and development and the meaning of behavior. These ideas are hard for many parents to understand. The difficulty in understanding is reflected in the not uncommon complaint that in the classrooms of such teachers the children "just play." Preschool teachers are under great pressure, sometimes openly, sometimes indirectly to prepare children for school. They are responsible to parents who naturally seek what to them is tangible, sensible evidence that they are in fact preparing children for the role of pupil."

It is the pressure thus applied to educators which hinders them from getting on with the business of teaching, or helping children acquire knowledge through experience—such as play. It is through play that the young child recreates the world and comes to understand it; his play is predicated on the experiences of his life and the explorations of his world. Unfortunately, the difference between what parents expect and what teachers want to try seems to be growing. Perhaps what we must do is educate parents as well as children; we have to help parents recognize that it is not that we are unconcerned about content, but rather that we approach content from a different direction and in different ways from the didactic system which they have come to expect and sometimes demand.

Often the parents' major concern is that their child will not be able to get a job, or make a living, or fulfill their professional expectations to be a success, unless they are equipped by the traditional didactic methods in a traditional classroom. Parents' pleasure with the early facts a child brings home from school—his ability to tell colors or count or recite the alphabet—and their encouragement of these activities and of behaviours which conform to classroom norms ("pay attention to the teacher, be a good child, be quiet in class, raise your hand"), suggest that specific content reduces their anxieties about their child's future. They do not understand that his future is in·fact extremely limited by the premature teaching of concepts typical of the traditional educational system.

Aside from the factors already mentioned, such as creativity and curiosity, we need to keep in mind that the world changes very quickly; a child didactically educated into some practical or professional role today will be seriously handicapped 20 years from now when much more knowledge, many more fields of study and work, will be available. Unless the child has developed ways of discovering, thinking, knowing and learning about things, he may be left hopelessly behind with his "old" knowledge. How many adults who grew up with the "old" math, for example, are either comfortable or competent with the "new" math unless it has been occupationally necessary for them to learn it? How many of us are even minimally knowledgeable about the concepts involved in computers, aside from using a word processor? With the rapid advancement of computer technology, someone who is only taught the basics of how to use one today, rather than the concepts on which computers operate, will possess hopelessly unusable information in 10 years, let alone 20!

We are better off teaching fewer "facts" and "truths" and "specific skills," and more awareness of the concept that knowledge increases almost daily, and that knowing how to access, process, synthesize, communicate, create new meanings for, and apply information is the key to being able to continually adapt and adjust to the ever-changing world. Our children, for all we know, may be living on the moon; a curious mind and the ability to feel free to explore will stand them in much better stead than the knowledge that there are, for example, a certain number of continents on the planet earth.

It is extremely important, therefore, that we do not allow ourselves as educators to be forced into the traditional role of "teacher as distributor of facts," control and content oriented, by the anxieties of the parents of the children we teach, who try to tell us that the earlier we "really teach" children, the better. It is hard to resist the pressure of the parents' group which insists that the money raised must buy, not a new adventure playground for the school yard, but computers for the grade 1 classroom. And it is difficult to discourage the well-meaning nursery or kindergarten volunteers who are determined to teach children to memorize the words in the picture book and call it reading, instead of reading the story to the children and talking about it with them, getting them to relate ideas or stories of their own which connect to it in their heads, and making up games and creating drama, music, and art activities which flow naturally from it. All of these activities would be far more beneficial to the child's language learning process than the premature memorization of sight words when the child doesn't possess the concepts needed to learn to read yet. So how do we stand firm, and teach in the ways we know are healthiest?

The answer, we think, is to evolve a well articulated and workable educational model for early childhood education and the primary years, with the developmental, educational, and psychological needs of the children as our first guideline. This must be quite specific in terms of the methodology and evaluation techniques to be used by teachers, the organization and atmosphere of the classroom, the connections between classroom activities and concepts to be learned, and the kinds of relationships we would like to see established between teachers and children to maximize both their academic and psychological growth. This model must be buttressed by the latest and most convincing research in the fields of education, sociology, and psychology, because it is only, unfortunately, such "scientific data and statistics" which might convince those pressuring for retention of, or return to, more traditional methods and subjects, and the addition of more rote learning and technological content in the early years of school.

We wish we could say, like stand-up comedians do, "And we just happen to have one right here!" as the water balloon is thrown out into the audience, but we don't—formulating such a model is not the work for any one person, but for the best minds in education across our society, for a vast number of teachers and students of all ages. But we do have some ideas about what we should like a classroom organized around such a model to be like, and we would like to share them with you, in hopes that they will stimulate some thought and discussion and disagreement and suggestions and writing on your part, so that such a model *can* be evolved for children who will live in the 21st century.

Perhaps we should make it clear right now what will *not* be part of any educational model we could support. There will *not* be rows and rows of desks in straight lines; rigid timetables with "subjects" in fifteen minute chunks; activities which require sitting quietly and absorbing "teacher talk" for long periods; dittos with pictures to color between the lines; brownie points or stars for neat handwriting, sitting still and being quiet ("being good"); mandatory recess activities decided upon and planned by the teacher; reading groups which mark out the "dumbies"; evaluation methods which label children as successes (winners) and failures (losers) for themselves, their peers, or their parents; lining up in tidy rows to move passively from one area of the school to another; mandatory handraising for all discussions; the lock step assumption that all children will, or can, learn the same information or skills at the same rate (the teacher's rate); singling children out in negative ways, or using sarcasm, belittlement, and exclusion from the group as punishment; questions asked only by the teacher, all of which have "one right answer"; and bulletin boards with only the "best" work, or the teacher's ideas, displayed. Did you think this kind of classroom had gone the way of the dinosaur? Look again!

Let's begin with a description of what a classroom might be like in a school organized around a new model. To do that, we return to sensory experience, the child's first hand exploration and manipulation of his world, as the key ingredient. The teacher influences these experiences by planning carefully for the achievement of desired goals and providing materials and increased opportunities for play. Materials such as blocks, easels and paints, fingerpaints, clay, fabrics, popsicle sticks, puzzles, large muscle toys, puppets, dolls, water, sand, lots of different sizes and colors of paper, and "found things" from the natural world are much in evidence. Trips to places in the neighbourhood and out, outdoor play in all seasons, watching artists or craftsmen at work, meeting "the people who work in our community", being exposed to music and dance and drama; these are all integral parts of the curriculum as well.

Children, alone, in pairs, and in small groups are involved with these materials, looking at books, playing dress up, listening to music or stories, talking to each other, playing pretend, or working on projects of some sort. Most of their activities involve manipulation and play with a wide variety of objects and materials so that the child can gain an awareness of what he can do, and what he needs or wants to learn, and then, with the teacher's guidance, is able to begin to do so. The child learns about form, size, sequence and texture by touching, looking, and comparing. He also learns about loudness, pitch, and clarity of sounds, by rattling, juggling, squashing, squishing and banging things on other things. He learns by smelling, and by associating various smells with certain activities, places, and people.

Throughout this process she begins to use language in a way that is meaningful to her—to discuss what she is doing, collecting, classifying, sorting, counting, pretending, or playing with her peers and the teacher, and to listen to them, responding to their feedback as cues for further activities and ideas and learnings. Language does not come about in a vacuum; it is a continually developing process which acquires importance only through contact with reality.

The teacher moves among them, watching, listening, questioning, providing a new material or idea, helping with a task which is giving trouble, recording children's stories for them, being an audience for a puppet play, cuddling an unhappy child in a corner, reading with a child, helping to organize materials or clean up, constantly alert for further opportunities to enrich the children's activities. She is no longer a person who only gives answers or solutions, or asks questions or assigns them from a book, but one who shares difficulties, provides resources, poses new problems for discovery, gives direction, and provides a role model for communication and learning.

The relationship between the child and the teacher is one of mutual respect; it is no longer one person who knows it all and another who learns, but rather one who guides and two who learn. Each teacher and child brings to school a unique identity made up of his or her cultural background, familial patterns and values, perhaps another language or religion, a learning style, and habitual ways of relating to others of the same age and other ages. It is the teacher's task to recognize and affirm the basic goodness and acceptability of each child's identity and to smooth the transition for the child, to adapt *to him* since he does not yet possess the capability of assessing the new reality of the classroom and rapidly adjusting himself *to it.*

As well, the relationship between teacher and child sharpens the child's self-awareness and helps her to recognize both the differences and the similarities between her and others. If others value her she values herself; she need not be discouraged then by the things she cannot do yet, or by lack of information. Safe in the acceptance she feels from her teacher, she can take risks and not feel "dumb" when she needs assistance; there is no clash between what she is "supposed to do" and what she *can* do because the teacher recognizes where she is at and understands her needs and her abilities. She can give her the freedom to explore, providing help, guidance, or criticism when necessary, but allowing her to find out ways of knowing things for herself.

The teacher recognizes that it is the individual child who is important, not the system, and that there is no one particular method to teach all children anything, but rather many ways of approaching a child. Her ability to relate to, support, and talk about each child as a unique and valuable person teaches them to be tolerant and understanding of each other; she does not create an atmosphere of competition to be "the best" or "the teacher's pet," but finds the strengths of each and helps them to share with and support each other so that they do not perceive things they cannot do as "bad." It is not often necessary to punish children in this classroom, because there are not a lot of rules made for efficiency's or the system's sake, or as tradition, or to maintain a tight structure; the child who wants to discuss an idea with others instead of sitting silently contemplating it as the teacher discusses it does not deserve punishment, but a flexible method which allows him to deal with an idea in ways which are meaningful to him.

There is a shift in this room from content rigidity to content openness; traditional subject areas are blurred, or do not exist anymore, since information from one is most certainly useful to another. Take, for example, an activity as seemingly "only playing" as using blocks. The growth of the child, not architectural masterpieces, is the first goal; physical release, body co-ordination, and emotional release through the dramatic use of blocks are involved. At first the child may work alone, enjoying the process of creating his own bridge or building; he may or may not want to talk about what he is doing. Later he begins to combine blocks and other play materials such as cars, trucks, clay, sand, or water, basing his dramatic play on the setting he creates. He may build a train station, for example, and then take imaginary trips either by himself or with others. He expands to take account of what those around him are building, perhaps working co-operatively to build a village. He may bring in materials, or make things in other areas of the room, such as clay animals or paper cutouts or popsicle stick trees or paintings to add to his creation.

The casual observer might feel that the child is "just playing," but look at the concepts she is rubbing up against! She is involved in language development as she discusses what to do next with others and makes up stories and playing-out situations; she is involved in primitive map-making as she lays out that train station or village or road; she is seeing for herself science concepts which she might not be able to deal with verbally for some time while using the wheel, ramp, pulley or lever, or discovering what shape block makes an arch balance and hold. She is also learning elementary physical and mathematical concepts about size and shape—"I need two more blocks"—"I need square blocks now"— "My train is longer than yours"—"This building is too tall so it falls down"—"All those blocks won't fit into this truck, it's too small."

It is important to realize that in this model the teacher does *not* simply say, "Let's do anything we want!" She guides and proposes projects which she recognizes as being helpful to a particular child at that moment, for a variety of physical, cognitive, or emotional reasons. The project is continually re-evaluated in terms of the child rather than the other way around, since she recognizes that as a child grows and synthesizes material there will be many plateaus and pauses, and some going back to simpler concepts on the climb to mastery of more complex activities. There may even be unconquerable mountains in a child's path—the learning disabled child for whom reading is nearly impossible, for instance. But she realizes that the child's self-image is developing out of his relationship with her and out of his explorations of the world, and that it needs nourishment, protection, and stimulation. If his self-picture is pretty healthy, the child sees himself as an exploring and curious person who is not too afraid, and he will learn; if he cannot view himself this way, then he does not learn—he may memorize, but he does not acquire skills which will enable him to go from one subject matter to another.

In the staff room of this new school, teachers will meet to discuss and question with an open attitude, to relate to each other as people, not just as teachers of particular subjects or classes whose closed classrooms are their own kingdoms, inviolable to criticism except from above by the occasional wandering consultant or administrator. They will feel free to move about, in and out of each other's rooms, to pool their strengths and teach each other new ways, to share ideas and materials, both those which worked and those which did not. Ideally, the children who will reach their rooms each year will not be strangers, or the infamous "behaviour problems" talked about disdainfully in staff lounges, but children they have worked with, talked to, and played with already in various multi-class and multi-age activities in the building.

The staff will be responsible as a group for making curriculum decisions, planning projects or units, discovering new resources, and ensuring the smooth transition of students from year to year, class to class, in the building; the principal will still be a teacher first and foremost, highly visible in classrooms and on the playground as an "encourager" not an "enforcer." Perhaps a rocking chair should be mandatory equipment for every principal's office, for the comforting of lost souls and the making better of scraped knees!

When it comes time to evaluate children in this classroom the questions are likely to focus on the quality of the relationship of teacher to child, the areas/concepts he is learning about, the things he has chosen himself to pursue, the learning style most functional for him, the kind of environment in which he is most comfortable, his social relationships with peers, his adjustment to the realities of school, the sense that adults have about his motivation, identity, anxieties, and strengths as a personality, whether assessments of his learning and skills are as accurate as possible, and whether there are specific concepts/learnings which need to be added to or removed from his curriculum. There is no beginning or ending of learning, so there is no "failure"—only areas which the next year's teacher will have to watch and support, when needed. The assumption is that each child has the potential to keep on learning and growing at a rate which is comfortable for him; and it is to that personal rate that the curriculum, and structures for teaching it, are adjusted accordingly.

If, one day in the year 2020, the adult who was your child is sauntering on the moon not far from his geodesic dwelling and sees a large purple animal with orange ears like germongous antennae, neon green whiskers, and suction cups for feet, jumping blithely through the air, and looking ever so much like a rabbit, what will be most valuable to him? The old definition of *rabbit,* memorized early in his school days and immortalized by endless spring dittos to color between the lines, as a soft white furry creature with a pink nose and fluffy tail and big feet who eats carrots and hops gently among the greenery (possibly carrying a large pastel straw basket full of lavender eggs!)? Or the ability to assess independently the "howness" of this new creature and decide, accordingly, whether to invite it home for tea or run like mad in the opposite direction?

Our children's ability to cope with the future may well depend on our ability as parents and educators to revise our long-held convictions and prejudices and habits and fears in time to change the educational system into a more open and exploratory way of learning and growing for all children, and for ourselves. We need to weed out the worst of the past from the classrooms of the present if we are to plant the seeds of a future in which our children can flourish.

PART TWO
PLAYING IS THE CHILD'S WAY
OF LEARNING ABOUT THE WORLD

Play—is there anything that apparently comes more naturally to children? Most of us can recall our parents saying, "what are you playing," "you can play after you finish eating," "will you please play somewhere else." But just what is play? There are undoubtedly as many definitions as there are kinds of play. For example, Collins *Dictionary of the English Language* list 39 different meanings of the word. However, one thing is for sure: play is definitely the "business" of childhood.

The three chapters in Part Two (chapters 5 to 7) of this book focus on the topic of play as a mechanism for allowing the child to explore and discover various aspects of the world. Chapter Five reviews some of the authors' developmental research on children's conceptions of play. Chapter Six examines how play serves to link the child's inner reality (imagination and fantasy) fantasies to his/her outer reality (real experiences in the world); the authors term this bridging of inner and outer reality—"cognitive map making." Chapter Seven explores the differences between imagination and pretend play, both of which serve to foster the child's cognitive or intellectual development.

Chapter 5

BUT WHAT *IS* PLAY, ANYWAY?

O ver the past twenty-odd years, a plethora of research and writing about play and children has issued forth from educational institutions, primarily in North America. Much of it has centered on the connection between children's play and their development, physically, cognitively, and emotionally. Psychologists in particular have observed children's play behavior, systematically described it, and evaluated the experiences seen in terms of the child's overall development. Perhaps coincidentally, this research emphasis happened at the same time as the push to teach children more, and earlier, as part of the great North American fixation on competition. Our children have to be brighter, better fed, more thoroughly lessoned and stimulated, than their age peers, and so the race to the best universities and the most lucrative careers begins with the mobile hanging over the newborn's crib.

Perhaps some of the research began as a defense mechanism, a way to try to convince the upwardly mobile parent to stay away from the flash cards for the 15 month old and let the child get on with his/her life; certainly much of the research indicated that play was one of the child's primary ways of learning about the world around him and where/how he fits into it. Perhaps some of it stemmed from a desire to refine toys in ways which would make them more 'educational' and thus of greater appeal to the anxious parent. Regardless of the reasons, however, all the research has one thing in common: it is the interpretive, subjective opinion of *adults*, albeit educated and objectively inclined, about what is in essence a very subjective, personal, individualized activity of *children*.

As there has been some difficulty arriving at a consensus regarding a definition of play, reflecting the different orientations of those conducting the research, methodological problems have arisen which may make generalizations from one study to another unwarranted. Thus to a great extent, how play is defined will determine the research focus, the questions asked and the conclusions arrived at, and unless the focus is the same, comparing the results may well be like comparing apples and oranges.

Our study was conceived as part of an effort to understand children's concepts of play—what is it, why do they do it, what activities fall into this category of experience? An earlier study (King, 1979, 1981) indicated that kindergartners interviewed say the most salient feature of play is that it is voluntary, and by grade five students regarded anything which was pleasurable, voluntary or not, as play; in addition, there was some shift from 'play is fun' in kindergarten to "play as work" in grade one.

There are, of course, some central problems in doing interview-based research with young children. The first of these is that wording the questions so that they aren't leading, but at the same time are clearly understood by young children, is very difficult; there really are no other words which mean "voluntary," for example, a term with which a five year old is unlikely to be familiar. The second of these is that children of this age (like many adults!) are uncannily likely to parrot what they have heard, or explanations they have been given, often without realizing that these "opinions" aren't really theirs. All you have to do is watch a handful of preschool or kindergarten children playing house, and saying the things they hear at home all the time to each other and to the dolls (occasionally to their parents' dismay when overheard!), to realize what a fine ear they have for oft-heard phrases.

The third, and perhaps the major problem, is that more than at any other age, they reflect the cultural/social class/educational level bias of their homes in terms of what they do in their spare time, what toys they own, where they are taken, how much TV they watch, and how much they are talked to about their experiences (as opposed to directed to do things). This is noticeable well into the early primary years, when the levelling effect of schooling plus peer contacts begins to affect them; often then it is possible to "hear" the teacher's voice in their explanations and answers as well as "see" the families and homes from which they come.

Our study, then, like any other done with young children, reflects these problems, and some of its findings may be questioned or explained in terms of them. But its findings are interesting nonetheless; perhaps they tell us as much about the way we tend to talk to children about play as they do about what children really think!

Twenty-five children from a largely middle to upper class, Caucasian background participated in this study; eleven in kindergarten (mean age, 5 years, 6 months, 3 females and 8 males) and fourteen in first grade (mean age, 6 years, 6 months, 9 females and 5 males). They were interviewed individually in a quiet room near the end of the school year by an experimenter who explained in advance that the purpose of the study was to discover what children could tell him about play and playing, and that the interviews would be taped because the interviewer would not be able to remember everything that would be said. The categories covered in the interviews were: the definition of play, reasons for playing, play as a learning experience, the fun of playing, the importance of play, home and school activities, and various levels of play—concrete/manipulative, representational/fantasy, and games with rules.

About 60% of the children overall defined play as *being* "fun," and about the same number said that they played *because* it was "fun." This would seem to be in contradiction to King's earlier findings that children identified the main attraction of play as being "voluntary," but on closer examination, these responses may not in fact be so far apart. It hinges on how the term "voluntary" is got across to a five year old, and on what, in fact, "fun" itself means at this age. Consider for a minute the circumstances under which play usually happens for children of this age: mum, busy and tired of kids underfoot and/or watching TV, says, "why don't you guys go outside and play for awhile?" or "turn off that TV and play, why don't you?" In either case, whatever the kids do next is likely to be out of sight and hearing of mum or any other adult who might want to put a damper on whatever activity is happening—no one tells them exactly what to do, how to do it, or supervises them.

Similarly, at school the harried teacher says at recess, "now go outside and play!" and again, a key part of what follows is that an adult doesn't tell them exactly what/how and stand around to make sure it gets done. Since the vast majority of the time an adult present in children's lives equals things that have to be done, and in a certain way, or with particular adult-imposed standards of neatness, quietness, and acceptability, the absence of these factors is central to "play" as it is experienced by most kids. So if kids had a larger vocabulary, perhaps we would discover that "fun" and "play" are synonymous terms to a large extent, and that central to both are the absence of adults, their rules, directions, and standards— play means you don't *have* to do it, or do it the grown up way, and we suspect this is so for many young children, whether they know how to say this to us or not.

This may also be why things that are *supposed* to be fun—like adult-organized games, or elaborate toys whose use mirror an adult reality— are so often ignored or discarded by kids. Remember the elaborate garage, airport, train or racing car set purchased at great expense, and overseen by a delighted dad full of instructions about how it *has* to be done or used—"no, the garage has to be right side up!"—but quickly abandoned by the four year old for the blocks which could be however his imagination wanted, while dad, grandpa, and the other grown-up boys played alone? Have you ever watched the five-year-olds, loaded to the shoulder pads and laced into skates, shoved out onto the ice to play out their fathers' fantasies of hockey stardom when they can barely stand up? This is supposed to be "fun," as are organized soccer and softball, but somehow the kids' faces often bear the resigned look familiar to class-room teachers just before the spelling test. Contrast this to the hours-long kids' games (an observant adult can watch them at a safe distance!), adult-free, hybrids with evolving rules to fit the size and age of their group, often with no "real" equipment except their imagination and bodies. Laughter, freedom, movement, pretending, other kids, no adults— these would seem to be central to what fun and play are all about.

Others of the responses are also open to interpretation: 20% of chil-dren reported that they wanted to play "to do something", but whereas those in kindergarten reported doing something with *something* (a toy, a bike), those in first grade more often reported doing something with *someone* (playing with friends, getting to know new friends). This find-ing indicates that play evolves from an activity primarily involving concrete manipulation to one involving socialization. However, it may also, given this particular population, reflect the realities of middle-class upbringing these days. Young children, especially those not yet in school, are often the only child (except perhaps a baby) at home, with lots of things to play with, but not many people. At that age they are unlikely to be allowed to go out to play farther than their own backyard, and many times even that equals solitary play.

Kindergarten teachers consistently report that they can spot the kids who didn't go to nursery school/day care, because they aren't used to sharing or playing with others comfortably. A large part of the excite-ment about going to school is the chance to meet other kids and have someone else to play with—by grade one, this sociableness is so marked that mothers of six year olds often go out of their way to "import" playmates on weekends and over holidays, since the same kids who could and would play alone happily for hours at four are bored stiff at six without playmates of their own age. So while this difference may be developmental, it may, in the suburban/urban life style, also be partially cultural in origin.

Kindergartners most frequently mentioned play as a learning experience in terms of the learning of physical skills, like riding a bike or rowing a boat (27%), of educational skills, like colouring, making a house (27%), and interpersonal skills, such as not pushing, not fighting, or getting along together (18%). This reflects not only the level of physical, large-muscle development expected at this age, but also the cultural and social expectations of the kindergarten environment. First graders mentioned the learning of educational skills, such as math, story writing, or learning to play instruments (43%), interpersonal skills, such as learning to be quiet, not being rough, and keeping on trying (28%), and skills required for future responsibilities, like fathering, mothering, and watching babies (28%).

Again, these reflect the changing priorities of the educational environment; whereas the kindergartners' activities are predominantly concrete, with no particular objective or goal in mind, those of the first graders are already geared toward that which is representational and academic.

These results also raise an interesting question: do adults, particularly teachers, try to connect "play", with all its favorable connotations for kids, and "learning," with all its favorable connotations for parents? The years following the Hall-Dennis Report's emphasis on education in the primary years, with play and experiential centres in nearly every classroom, were mirrored by some articles and books (Barth, 1970; Dearden, 1968; Ridgeway and Lawton, 1968; Marsh, 1970) of the late 60's and 70's which seemed to be interpreted as giving permission to "just let kids play and learn by themselves"; and most of today's primary teachers began teaching then.

In the past few years, however, the emphasis on "back to the basics" and "early learning" have been important parent buzz-words; nursery schools which offer second language learning at three, day camps which include computers for the four year old, massive sales of "educational" books, toys, and records—all may have had an impact of an unexpected nature on primary teachers. Now all of a sudden "just playing" seems not to be as acceptable to parents, who want signs of "real learning"—it is not unusual to find a parent demanding written homework for their grade one child—but many teachers, after years of working with primary children, are convinced of the value of imaginative and creative play as an education in itself and as the best method of socialization available to the classroom in particular and to the school system overall.

So maybe what is happening is that as teachers let children play, they verbalize what they perceive as what children learn from that particular play activity—"we're playing this game so that you'll learn about sharing (or numbers, or remembering names, etc.)." Perhaps children, listening to their parents' explanations—"we got you this game so you could learn all about dinosaurs"—have also come to expect some 'learning agenda' from what would otherwise be play activities. Somehow "just playing" is almost a waste of time, even in the eyes of the young middle class child—"we weren't doing anything important, we were just playing"—"we didn't do anything on the holiday, we just played around."

The older kids get, the more clearly this is seen; drama, art, music and physical education classes in upper elementary/junior high years suffer from the stigma of "not really learning anything—we just play around" to the point that teachers of these subjects occasionally destroy the process and inject "real" learning—writing, drills, tests, projects that are marked—as a stern reminder and because otherwise "the kids won't work—they just have fun!"

Re-enforcement of this hypothesis might be found in the children's responses to the questions about the role play has in their development; 32% of the kids interviewed report that it is important for physical well-being, 32% as a learning experience; 16% for socialization, and only 8% for fun. We can't see, somehow, the average five year old saying to a friend, "let's go out and play because it will make us strong and healthy"—or "then we'll be able to get along better." These sound an awful lot more like adult echoes—"get away from that TV and get outside and play so you'll be strong and healthy" (sub-text: and give me some peace and quiet, and make sure you'll go to sleep at a decent hour tonight!) Or, "we'll play this card game, but you know we're really learning our math skills this way"—or "you have to include everyone in your tag game at recess because you have to learn to get along with all the children."

An interesting trend revealed by the responses was the move toward play as an activity reflecting pretense and imagination. In kindergarten, physical activities, crafts, and toys are prominent activities, with pretense a more minor activity; by grade one, imagination and pretense activities were the most prevalent, followed by toys, physical activities, games, and crafts. It would be interesting to see if this difference were as marked in a group of children who had all had nursery school experiences before kindergarten; in other words, is it a product of age development, or of experience with other children, socially and at play?

We divided the responses into concrete, representational, and game categories and compared them not only on an age basis but in terms of home vs school. Again, the responses may be read in terms of what is available in each location—toys and people—as well as indicating developmentally profound differences. At school, on a concrete level, kindergartners played more with blocks than with toys; it was the reverse in grade one. This suggests that the younger children enjoy play which requires concrete manipulation and the older prefer that which involves a more abstract, mental, or imaginative factor. It also may reflect the general availability of giant block sets in kindergartens but not often in grade one classrooms, where more of the space is allocated to desks and shelves on which smaller toys and games are easily accommodated. This is borne out by the lack of such distinction in play at home, where toys are mentioned by both, and blocks not at all; big block sets are very expensive and cumbersome for home use!

On a representational level, kindergartners report involvement in crafts and first graders in pretense/imagination activities. At home, both mention pretense, and crafts are not mentioned. This certainly reflects the emphasis on small muscle art/craft activities—drawing, finger painting, making pot holders, working with clay—which are the mainstay of the more quiet times in a kindergarten class, and which are not as often part of parents' home supplies, as they require more supervision/care and sometimes are messy. But "playing pretend" is either a solitary or a group activity requiring little but the imagination.

On a game level, the younger children mention physical activities like bike riding, but limited mental skill games, and no organized sports at school. By first grade games are more prominent than individual physical activities, but sports are beginning to appear too. At home both groups most frequently mentioned individual physical activities, with some sports at the kindergarten level and a wide involvement in games like checkers at the first grade level. Again this may mirror different conditions at home; one or two children of varying ages in a family are likely to be sent to their playroom/outside with a ball or a bike until they are perceived as old enough to play quietly with a board game—but obviously this requires the availability of another kid near the same age or a willing parent, too.

Taken overall, these results are consistent with previous knowledge about interests and capabilities of children on a developmental continuum. Younger children seem to be attracted to/involved in play focusing on physical activities of some sort, whereas within a year or so of entering school, children are more involved in abstract types of activities as well. We might want to generalize by saying that the older children are predominantly concerned with the abstractness of *thinking* about play, while the younger children are mostly concerned with the concreteness of *doing* it.

In the spirit of questioning, however, we feel compelled to ask if this is a chicken/egg situation; the discrepancies between home and school responses, and our knowledge of the typical culture of the middle class family vis a vis child raising and toy buying habits, indicate that it may be. *If* the toys and social contacts available at home and school were more nearly identical, and children were all in classrooms equipped like nurseries/kindergartens until age 7 or so, would we see the same differences in activities/interests? Do the interests change as parents and teachers provide different kinds of activities/toys and varying contexts and nudges/comments/instructions? Or are the changes in interests there first, and parents and teachers respond by providing the necessary equipment, context, and reinforcement? This is of course a very difficult if not an unanswerable question, but one which should make us think a little about our assumptions about play and how they translate into what we make available in schools and at home.

An interesting sidelight is the children's perceptions of when play is "*Not* fun": where there is physical abuse, a lack of compromise in the decision about what is happening, or a lack of people to play with. It is seen as boring if it is too hard in terms of skills or ideas, or lacking in variety. These are certainly quite reasonable qualifiers—most adults would view recreation with these qualities as "not fun" too! Some of these are by-products of kids' initial socialization attempts, like the inability to compromise when one is used to playing alone, or the tendency for kids to become frustrated and hit out, especially compounded by differences in age or size, or the addiction to having others to play with once they're used to it which is so typical of kids in the primary years. Some of them are all too typical of the 'educational' games as loved by grandparents—

the ones with copious instructions and "knowledge" packed in there, like the board game entitled "Class Struggle" given to a ten-year-old of our acquaintance. These really aren't fun at all, because they're designed for adult interests, skills, and attention spans.

In spite of the qualifications discussed already, it seems clear that the sequence of play development seen here proceeds from play involving primarily motor activity and concrete manipulations, to play involving the ability to represent activities, objects, and events mentally, to play where the child begins to engage in interaction with other children and an adherence to rules. Younger children seem to simply play, and their games do not seem to have any rules or penalties for infractions of rules. In contrast, the games of older children seem to be regulated by rules and there are winners and losers. It may be that play involving motor activity and concrete manipulation may be necessary for imaginative play to occur, and in turn for social play to develop. In particular, social play requires not only that one knows how to manipulate objects and respect rules, but it also requires social skills in order to interact with other children.

The sequence of development suggested by these results is consistent with Piagetian theory. The young child is aware of the external, directly perceivable aspects of events and objects, while the older child is more aware of the abstract, conceptual aspects of objects and events. According to Flavell (1977), the younger child is prone to accept things as they seem to be in terms of their outer, perceptual, phenomenal, on-the-surface characteristics. The older child seems to be more sensitive to the basic distinction between what seems to be and what really is, i.e., between the phenomenal and the apparent, and the real and the true. Case (1983) suggests that as the child develops, the focus of the child's thought changes. As the child matures, he gradually becomes capable of focusing on two, three, and later four relationships. With each step, the new structures increase in complexity and are qualitatively distinct from the earlier structures. The sequence of development that has been described in this study is a function of the developing cognitive abilities (Khanna, 1984).

It is apparent that initially, play is restricted to the element of physical activity, however, as the child evolves, play seems to become inclusive, that is, it begins to include the element of mental activity. Eventually, as the child develops greater cognitive capacities, play evolves and gradually becomes perceived as an educational method, a way of learning various skills including those related to physical fitness, socialization, and future responsibilities (Weininger, 1984).

Whether these are purely age-dependent developments or also experience-dependent cannot be seen from this study; it would require a far larger group of children, beginning perhaps at four and continuing until ten or so, and would need to look separately at children who attended nursery school before kindergarten. It would also be helpful if the children came from a wider range of social classes, and perhaps if a range of families in terms of the number and ages of siblings and of a variety of locations (urban, suburban, rural, non-western cultures, etc.) were considered.

This study proves useful in affirming, then, some ideas researchers have had about the developmental nature of play. It is less useful in terms of its stated purpose—to understand *children's* concepts of play—because of the problems mentioned at the beginning in terms of question design and semantics, and because of the small group size and the homogenous quality of the children studied. Children's vocabularies and ability to verbalize an abstract like "play" or "fun" are limited, and once again, it requires adult interpretation to reach an analysis. The question of "What is play?" leads only to other questions: what, to a child, is "fun"? What does adult supervision or direction have to do with either or both of these? How much of what kids say about play, especially in terms of what they learn from it, is their unconscious parroting of their parents' and teachers' rationales/directions?

We are left with the idea that children *see* play as fun, and play *because* it is fun—but any parent or older child could tell us that without a study! So perhaps there is no method by which adults bent on research can expect a careful behavioural/emotional/cognitive definition with which to begin from the subjects themselves. If, as adults, we want to study children and play, we are still going to have to begin with the same old question—"But what IS play, anyway?"

Chapter 6

CHILD'S PLAY AS COGNITIVE MAP MAKING

A deep connection links inner and outer reality for children—the inner, their intellectual and emotional life, and the outer, their experiences with people and the real world in which they live—and the way that children accommodate to this real world is through play. The pioneering work of Susan Isaacs in the field of children's play (1930, 1933, 1950) has lent a considerable base to this philosophical belief, and, in her opinion, "play is the child's means of living and of understanding life" (1930). The child is, essentially, formulating a personal schema, his own cognitive map, which enables him to begin to understand the world about him in more or less objective terms.

Play evokes thought, language, and activity; it permits the child to deal with her intellectual processes in a way which makes these processes acceptable, and accessible, to her. When it is not forced, rigid, restricted, or circumscribed, it allows her to structure her world, using language, gestures, body movements, and the objects in her environment. No other activity motivates, nor permits a child to find out about herself, as well as play. It is, in fact, "the most complete of all educational processes, for it influences the intellect, the emotions, and the body of the child." (Scarfe, 1962).

Just as the previous chapter discussed the need to have a clear understanding of what we mean by play, it is necessary here to digress for a moment and consider what we mean by the familiar phrase, "cognitive development." This is by no means as obvious as it seems. In a 1983 study, Cairns reviewed the history of the science of behavioural development and found an interesting diversity of theoretical and methodological approaches stretching back over the last one hundred years. Case (1984) commented on the major traditions within this history and identified them as the empiricist, rationalist, and historico-cultural. The following summaries of these traditions are adapted from a recent article by Eckler and Weininger (1989).

The roots of the empiricist tradition lie in the writings of Locke and

Hume, who postulate that knowledge acquisition is a process in which the human perceptual system detects events or stimuli in the external world, and the cognitive system detects patterns and makes sense of such information. Those who subscribe to this theory tend to view intellectual development as the child's increasing ability to make associations between stimuli. These ideas have led to behaviourist and neo-behaviourist theories, and, more recently, information processing theories. These theories share an assumption that information provided by the senses is at the basis of all knowledge, and thus that learning and development are essentially equivalent.

The rationalist tradition has its roots in the philosophy of Kant, an approach emphasizing reason as the primary source of knowledge, before, more important than, and independent of sensory perception. Kant felt that knowledge is acquired by the imposition of order on sensory data, not merely by any vague quality detected in such data. Within this tradition intellectual development is viewed as age-related changes in an ability with which humans are equipped from birth; the impact of physical and social experience are minimized in this view. Clearly Piaget's work on what he perceived as largely invariant stage changes in human development is the foremost research based on this philosophical approach.

The writings of Goethe, Hegel, and Marx provide the source for the historico-cultural tradition. This view postulates that knowledge is always acquired in a social context as a function of unique historical circumstances. Intellectual, cultural, and social experience are inseparable from the social and physical environment and from the coping skills developed by human beings to deal with their world. The theories of Vygotsky (1962) and Bruner (1965) are the best known of those who work within this tradition; Bruner, for example, felt that growth of the mind is always growth assisted from the outside.

Flavell (1978) wrote about the "theory of cognitive development we are all waiting for" whose rather ironic purpose was to suggest that none of the definitions arising out of research in any of the three areas outlined above gives a complete picture. Each of them contains thought-provoking ideas and is based on observation and common sense, and each can be seen as being a philosophical approach to the nature of the human mind as much as a psychological theory.

What is very clear from the above summary is that we do not have a definition of cognitive development on which we can all agree; if we are honest we might recognize that this debate may well be the

modern metaphoric equivalent of the medieval debate on how many
angels might dance on the head of a pin! We may never, by any scientifi-
cally valid method, be able to establish the exact nature of cognitive
development, much less separate out its sensory, processing, experiential,
and adaptive components. For purposes of research into the relationship
between play and cognitive development, it is perhaps safest to make
clear from which particular tradition one perceives the latter. In the case
of "cognitive map making" as it was first used, one might assume that the
definition falls largely into the empiricist framework.

"Cognitive maps" is a term originally devised by E. C. Tolman in 1948,
and it was used primarily to indicate the knowledge that an individual
had of his or her real life space. Tolman suggested that an individual was
able to formulate a construct which was "an overview of the spatial
relationship comprising a special space." It did not seem to Tolman that
the cognitive map was a simple memory process of specific spatial
relationships, like turning right or left, or "there is a chair here and a
table there," but rather, that the individual was able to construct in his
own thinking a comprehensive map of an area. The cognitive map was a
generalized view of spatial relationships within a given space. A "strip
map" would then be a more detailed mapping of a specific region within
the comprehensive map.

For a child, then, this means that he may be fully aware that the dining
room in his house has a table, six chairs and a buffet, a lamp overhead, a
rug on the floor, and a window with curtains. The strip may contain, for
him, the details of the rug pattern under the table which he has used as a
road route for his toy cars. He has a detailed spatial understanding of the
space under the table, which for him is very meaningful and becomes
organized and understood because of his frequent play there. The comprehensive map permits him to orient himself within the room and to be
casual in the use of movement in getting around it; he doesn't have to
actively *think* about how to move around the room so as not to hit a piece
of furniture, for example (Siegel & Schadler, 1977).

We would like to suggest, however, that the concept of a cognitive map
can usefully be expanded to serve as a metaphor for the child's way of
bridging inner and outer reality, of accommodating her thoughts, feelings,
and fantasies to the realities she experiences in early childhood, and that
the major tool for such map-making is a child's play.

At most times in the child's life her cognitive map will contain not
only the real objects in the space, but will be elaborated upon by imagina-

tion and fantasy. Fantasy will be used by the child to complete the map when there are details missing which are required in order for her to achieve satisfaction at that moment within her environment. The child may not separate fantasy and reality ideas or experiences on her map, and it will appear as though she doesn't understand the difference between the two, or is making mistakes; but in fact it is not a mistake, because this distortion of reality was needed in an effort to try to gain satisfaction from her world.

When the child plays she is using fantasy, which becomes reality as she plays; when she realizes the playing does not conform to adult reality, the fantasy slowly changes, and this can be observed as shifts in the child's play. The role of thinking, perception, comprehension, and re-evaluation become important as tools permitting the child to make use of play to correct the fantasy and bring it into line with the real experiences in her life. These three functions—perception, comprehension, and re-evaluation—are the ingredients of her later capacities to use intelligence; that is, through play the child is formulating the foundation for potential use of intelligence.

There are also aspects of a child's cognitive map-making that are within the realm of the unconscious. Piaget (1973) has pointed out that the "cognitive structure is the system of connections the individual can and must use, and can by no means be reduced to the contents of conscious thought." Piaget also notes that "the cognitive unconscious thus consists in an ensemble of structures and of functions unknown by the subject except in their results." Piaget is pointing out that certain aspects of the child's functioning in terms of problem-solving and awareness of his environment are conscious, and in part an ego function, but that all of his problem solving and awareness are not on a conscious, ego-cognitive level. The structure of the environment is backed up by responding directly to it; responding to it in a pre-conscious or not fully aware level, and responding to it in an unconscious way.

Thus it is not unusual, if we ask a young child to draw a map of his room, for him to leave out certain aspects of it. If we ask him questions about this, he will add those details which our questions stimulate; this is the result of pre-conscious cognitive awareness. If we ask him to solve certain kinds of problems about his room, depending of course on his level of development, the child will not only make use of the map that he has drawn to solve the problem, but will ferret out from his unconscious those parts of the room which he had left out which only became available to him as he solved the problem. Thinking and cognitive structure in map-making are not, then, entirely a conscious affair. Experiences, including physical actions, sensory motor play, and observations of things, all help in the formulating of the cognitive map.

While this assimilation of the unconscious is part of the play process, so is direct learning. During play the child explores, and experiments directly with, the thoughts, ideas, and understandings he has of his inner and outer world, and this in turn allows him to build his inner world a little closer to the outer reality. The child picks pieces of his environment— home, classroom, and neighbourhood—and plays with them in what may seem to an adult a poorly-organized fashion. He leaves this bit, picks up another, plays with it, looks at the play of other children, returns to the original bit, and by this ongoing process of accommodation and correction, gradually brings it all together into a meaningful whole for himself.

While the child is involved in cognitive map making, she is also developing schemata which seem to permit her to be creative. The broader the schema which she acquires by exploration and curiosity while playing with a wide variety of objects and materials, the greater the creativity which results. The following observation of three little girls at play demonstrates the ways in which this seems to happen.

The girls were making an outline of a house using small blocks; they had already formed several rooms, put in furniture, and were looking for babies and families to occupy the house. One of them moved away from this outlined house, found a piece of paper and a pencil, and made a picture of a person. It was suggested that if they made all their people with paper, crayons, and scissors they could have the number and the size they wanted. As they did this, they noticed a box of materials nearby, and it was suggested that one piece was pretty and might make a nice dress for the mother. So they began making clothes for all their paper dolls, and were joined by another girl who brought beads, with which they started to make jewellery.

A little boy came over, watched for a bit, and suggested that they needed a big bed for the family, and that he would make it. Using paper, cardboard, and scissors, he fashioned a rather effective large bed for the whole family. The five children now began to play "family," left their craft work and started to role- play members of the family they had created. After about ten minutes, one child took a paper and pencil and said she was going to leave a message for her mother, and began to write;

the others also started to write messages. This prompted another child to say that the house needed a letter box to post their letters in, and this was created too.

Thus the original house, the paper dolls, the clothing, beads, family role-playing, and letter box all came together, forming an effectively functioning schema for these five children. This permitted them to explore several situations within their own families, within their own individual fantasies, and within their peer interactions. It was a very effective two hour learning for them, as it permitted each of them a greater understanding of family functions and peer co-operation, as well as extending their writing, language, and social skills.

Piaget (1952) sees the development of such schemas as, at first, egocentric and later as assimilating into operational stages and contributing to intellectual development as the child actively incorporates the external world into his ego. At first, a child is essentially an egocentric person who feels that because he knows something, it must be true and correct; this makes it difficult for him to accept information from other people. Through play, this egocentric position is gradually changed to one where a child is more able to incorporate the ideas and information of others, not only peers but also parents and teachers. Thus the processes of play and socialization are an integral part of a child's psychological maturation.

Play is also a very valuable component of language development in young children. During play, the child uses speech to verbalize what she is doing; her vocabulary is increased, and she is more able to talk freely and communicate ideas to others, by the participation in activities with a wide variety of objects, materials, and people. As Susan Isaac writes, "words are only tokens of experience, and are either empty or confusing to children until they have had enough immediate experience to give the words content. With young children, words are valueless unless they are backed by the true coin of things and doings. They have their own place as aids to experience, and to clear thought about experience" (1930).

The child manipulates objects and words to make order out of her world; through sensitive listening and questioning, the adults around her aid her language development by encouraging the extension and expansion of the language she is using in her play. A child needs to find her sense of logic and reasoning by communicating to others the structure of the world she is creating through her play. It is almost as though play creates the opportunity for pre-verbal logical thinking and working out of understandings, and then allows a child to verbalize her reasoning and logic. Play is the stage that permits the initial activity to unfold, and carries along with it the seemingly separate functions of language and reasoning. These are not, in reality, separate functions, since language encourages reasoning because it helps the child to recognize what others think of her speech efforts; their non-understanding causes her to struggle to clarify and re-organize, or to find better words, to make herself understood.

In playing, the child finds herself and gains a sense of satisfaction and competency, as well as some recognition of the uniqueness of her own individual methods of expression and her own creativity. It allows her to explore feelings, to recreate situations which are difficult or dangerous for her, to deal with "as if" situations without getting so involved that she can't extricate herself. She can explore what it feels like to be a policeman, a teacher, or Superman, and she can gain temporary satisfaction trying out the role of a boy, a mother, or a father as she gradually learns her own role, that of a child and a girl in her family. It is the best way for her to integrate all of her experiences and make sense out of all the things which happen to her, or that she feels, during a day.

Play also has the power of relieving a child of anxiety and turmoil, allowing him to absorb information which might have been threatening or dangerous. For example, two children playing "going to the hospital to have my tonsils out" are playing out a potentially anxious time in a young child's life with all the information they possess—from their family, the doctor, TV shows, and previous medical procedures—to make it safer. And after the fact, the child who was hospitalized may continue to "play doctor" until all the parts he didn't understand seem to come together in his own mind, and the experience is made part of his cognitive map.

Play, then, has a multitude of functions in the personal, individual development of each young child; it helps to alter egocentrism, to evolve a functional base for intellectual pursuits, to increase creativity and self-expression, to develop language skills, and to relieve anxiety, and it permits a child to integrate these various functions over time by the creation of an increasingly complex cognitive map. Play is, in fact, the learning base not only for childhood but also for adult life. It is also the base of the socialization necessary to any civilization, which is firmly imbedded in interactions not only with the adults, family and

teachers, of a child's world, but with other children; children observe
and stimulate each other in different ways than do adults. As important
as the mother, or caregiver, is to the development of the young child, it is
clear that in childhood contact, interactions, and play with peers enhance
a child's social development (Saltz and Johnson, 1974; Strain & Weigernik,
1976).

When does cognitive map-making, and the play which is its external
ramification, begin in young children? Traditionally many have felt that
this kind of behaviour begins around the age of two, but we suspect
that it is much earlier, perhaps almost from birth. The pleasure which a
baby exhibits when being fed, cuddled, and kept warm, and by responding
to soft sounds, particularly cooing sounds made by his mother, might be
considered the first aspects of play, as they permit an equilibrium to
develop between the child and his environment. This is a necessary
pre-condition to an orderly cognitive functioning, a learning process
which permits the growth of basic neurological processes and psychological characteristics, and the infant who is not provided with such basic
care and mothering does not evolve or develop effectively.

The infant not only spends time trying to achieve this equilibrium, or
homeostatic state, but when it is achieved, involves himself in a kind of
passive looking and listening. We have all seen an infant lying very still
and staring intently at its mother's face or a brightly coloured or moving
object, or seeming to concentrate for some time on a soft sound. This passive state appears to permit the infant to connect and interrelate such things
as mother's voice and food; mother's voice and a teddy bear, mother's
touch and mother's smile. All these connections constitute the beginning
of his cognitive map, which brings activities and experiences together
for the child. Essentially, pleasure and subsequent homeostatis permit
passive staring and listening, then act as the urge toward activity on the
part of the infant, to select stimuli and to respond to them. This helps the
infant to gather those stimuli which mean mother, which permits him to
begin the difficult process of object constancy; gradually the mother
becomes a whole object, an image fixed in the cognitive map of the child.

As the baby grows older, he explores larger sections of his environment,
at times looking at things in great detail, at others looking about in a
kind of total scan. At this point, it seems important for the baby to have
an interesting environment and to have toys which are appropriate for
his age and maturational level. As his exploration continues, satisfaction
occurs because the activity is intrinsically rewarding for the baby. He

doesn't need external encouragement or reward, but he does need an environment which encourages such explorative play.

As a child becomes a moving person, creeping and crawling, his cognitive maps become extended, including not only physical aspects of his environment, but tactile, auditory and kinesthetic stimuli which provide greater detail for his maps. Sounds of activities become more meaningful and he can now predict what is going on, where it is going on and how long he might have to wait alone. This is an important and urgent experience for the infant and young child to undergo, for it permits him to evolve an ego function of delay in gratification, to withstand frustration and to recognize that mother will be here soon, but not right now, to satisfy his needs.

This kind of interrelating of various stimuli, sensory and motor, help him to bring together and integrate various kinds of experiences. As soon as he can manage to do so, everything gets put into his mouth, and these oral activities are integrated with the various other stimuli. We think it is at this point in his life, about 6 to 8 months of age, that a child begins to develop a special cognitive style of his own—his own way of thinking, acting, playing—to learn about his world. He is responding with his own internal structures—thinking processes, feeling states—to the people and objects of his environment through this cognitive style, and it, in turn, is expressed by his cognitive map-making.

At the same time as the baby is being curious about the objects he can see, feel, touch, smell and taste he is learning how to handle his body. Watch a baby determinedly trying again and again until he manages, suddenly, to turn over—and then, with a glance at mum to see if she shares his triumph, does it again and again. The same process is followed to get his tummy off the floor for his first good crawl, and then to push and pull himself to a stand on a piece of furniture or the side of his crib. He examines his fingers and toes and knees carefully, as if trying to assess exactly what each is good for; clearly this is part of the formation of his body image and of gaining control over motor skills.

Sometimes he is hurt at doing this—he falls, bumps his head, scratches himself--and often the look of surprise is quite clear on his face just before the enraged and frustrated howl! It is as if his pride is involved, and he can't believe he couldn't do it, but this in turn teaches him that pain can be avoided by increasing or improving his dexterity. He develops more "fail-safe" strategies for avoiding pain, and these are often more creative than his first attempts. For example, I (Ms. Daniel) watched a baby trying to master crawling up a small flight of stairs; he fell two or three times, and then appeared to give up, but later that afternoon I saw him climbing from the bottom mattress to the top one of his brothers' trundle bed in their shared room. He fell again, but persevered and finally learned to coordinate hands and knees so that he could do this smoothly, and then shot me a look of incredible triumph! That evening, with his mother close behind him on the way to his bath, he crawled slowly but without falling up the stairs. Clearly he had learned a coping strategy that day!

It is as though motor function, sensory function, ego systems, homeostatis and cognitive development all occur in and about the same time. While we may talk about these aspects of her life as though they are separate, it is essential to think about them as being integrated and functioning in reciprocal fashion. This kind of reciprocity allows the child to go ahead in one specific skill, holding others in abeyance, so when she walks it seems as though she does not talk as much, but once walking is mastered, talking comes back at its original, if not a greater, level than before. Her improvement in all these competencies allows her to create strategies to avoid being bored, looking further afield in her environment for things which will satisfy her curiosity and allow her to use her newly honed skills. Curiosity is an intrinsic characteristic of the young child's approach to her world, and it leads her into the contacts with others besides her family, through play and communication, which are critical for the socialization process.

As a child grows from infancy to pre-schooler, her need for involvement with others also grows, and her play behaviour progresses through five stages: solitary, spectator, parallel, associative, and co-operative play (Smilanksy, 1968). Most of the exploratory sensory-motor activities described thus far are part of the solitary play stage, which usually lasts for about two years. During this stage, the child is very content to play solely on her own, and all parents have to do is provide access to a variety of interesting objects and try to keep hazardous things out of her reach. Play with anyone else at this stage tends to be of the peek-a-boo, patty-cake, five-little-piggies, and knee-bouncing-to-songs variety engaged in with adults, as much for their pleasure as the child's!

Spectator play may occur at any age during childhood, but it is most noticeable in the baby who is content to sit in her stroller and just watch the activities going on around her—much like the staring at mother and near objects she did in the first months of life. Older children may stand

and watch if they don't feel secure about their position with those they are watching, but they would eagerly join if invited.

In parallel play, two-year-olds pursue their individual activities in the presence of other children without any seeming interest in each other, even if they are close to each other in the room. They still seem largely absorbed in the individual process of exploring the things in their environment, although occasionally younger siblings of this age will change this pattern and demand whatever the older child is playing with. I watched a 3½ year old cope with this problem very cleverly; he would go to the toy box and choose a toy carefully (never one of his current favourites) and proceed to play with it with great noise and flurries of activity, totally involved with it. His 2-year-old sister would watch for awhile, and then move over and quite assertively grab it; he knew he wasn't allowed to hit the baby, so he would give it up, but with every evidence of dismay. She would take the toy to her play space and try to do with it the things he had been doing, usually not very successfully, but totally absorbed. Then he would go and take the toy he really wanted and play with it quietly, out of her line of sight if possible. Clearly he had learned some valuable coping strategies!

By three years of age, associative play is generally observed; although each child engages in his own activity, some interaction and simple exchanges go on between them. Frequently they exchange information about the equipment they are using or the pretending they are doing, although frequently the connections between their statements are difficult for an adult to keep track of. This is the stage of "my truck goes faster than yours" and "I have a dolly, but you don't have one" in which play occasionally comes to blows.

Between the ages of four and five, attempts at co-operative play become more evident, particularly in children in nursery, daycare, and junior kindergarten settings. This kind of play requires an acceptance of mutual roles in the play, and its success depends on each child co-operating and carrying out the obligations implied by the role he has taken. The little girl who imperiously announces to her playmate that "babies aren't allowed to talk" when they are playing house, for example, will probably lose "baby," as it is difficult for young children to accept their chosen (or assigned) roles for very long, especially if theirs is not of major importance in the play. These early attempts at co-operative play often fail and result in quarrels, physical aggression, and tears, along with "he started it, mummy!" The social skills necessary for totally successful co-operative play are acquired gradually through the pre-school and primary years, and can probably not develop well unless children have ample opportunities for self-selected play, as opposed to adult-regulated games.

It is through this five or six year progression, from earliest infant sensory explorations to co-operative play, that a child develops the cognitive map which allows him to define himself, make sense out of the world he lives in, and perceive how he best fits into it. Play permits the child to learn about learning, to form a cognitive foundation for subsequent learning of academic skills and concepts, as well as to teach him the interactive and co-operative personal and social skills which are part of human society.

Child's play is an instinctive, often autonomous and wholly absorbing pursuit with long term social and collective repercussions, for it teaches a child what no one else can teach him. To recollect our metaphor, it is as if the cognitive map which he crafts for himself through play over the early years not only shows where the bridges between his inner and outer lives are, but also indicates where and how the bridges between himself and other people are to be built, in order that he too may come to realize that "no man is an island, entire unto himself."

Chapter 7

"WHAT IF" AND "AS IF":
IMAGINATION AND PRETEND PLAY
IN EARLY CHILDHOOD

Patrick, just three, decided one day that he was going to use "imagination" to bake a cake. He announced that to do this he would need flour, eggs, baking powder, sugar, salt, marshmallows, and chocolate chips, and that the cake would have to go into the microwave oven to cook. Smiling, his mother agreed, assuming that he intended to pretend all these ingredients and play at baking a cake. But after listing these ingredients for her, he went into the kitchen, sat himself up at the counter, and began to ask her to get the ingredients he would need. He decided he needed the biggest bowl and a stirrer, and would need the flour first. His mother asked how much he needed, and Patrick responded, "About one cup." After receiving this, he poured it into the mixing bowl and asked for the baking powder, but seemed a bit puzzled. So his mother said, "We usually only use a little bit of baking powder," and Patrick said, "I need only a little bit too." His mother suggested a teaspoon and he agreed this was about right. The rest of the ingredients followed, in much the same fashion, until he stopped and said that he would have to use his imagination again. After a few seconds of reflection, Patrick announced that all he needed was an egg and some water.

After he added these and stirred everything, he put the mixture into a baking pan and put it in the microwave with his mother's help. He wanted to know how long it should stay there and his mother replied, "It looks as if it needs about five minutes." Patrick agreed that was just the right amount of time. When the cake came out, Patrick was obviously delighted and set it on the windowsill to cool while he watched, smiling.

Patrick was using his imagination and to him, as well as to many other young children with whom we have worked, there is a great difference between "imagination" and "pretend." When a young child uses imagination, he or she is thinking about solutions to various problems he or she has perceived; so when Patrick announced he would use "imagination" to make a cake, he was thinking, silently and out loud, about what he would need, and what the process would be, in order to do this.

Imagination *is* different from pretend, although the two are intimately connected in the ongoing interactive process of thoughts and actions in a child's intellectual development. *Imagination* is to the young child what problem solving is to the adult. *Pretend* is another activity altogether: it is play, the kind of play that usually has a theme that often involves other people, either children, dolls, or "pretend people" (Weininger, 1982).

The following episode should make clear the difference between these two activities, imagining and pretending. Three year old Hillary went to the housekeeping centre to play "a tea party." She talked aloud as she set the table and the tea cups and the spoons, saying, "We are going to have milk and cookies," as she placed two empty plates on the table. Then she set the chairs at the table, saying, "These are for the mommy, the daddy and the baby brother." Off she went to gather two other children to come and play "tea party" with her. When the threesome came together at the table, Hillary announced, "I'm the girl and you are the mommy and you are the baby brother." The two other three-year-olds accepted their roles, sat down according to her instructions and all three began to play:

Hillary: You have milk in your tea, Mommy.
Mother: Yes, but we need to have cookies.
Hillary: They are on the table, don't you see them in the brown plate?
Mother: Oh yes, but I like big fat cookies.
Hillary: Well then, they are big fat cookies.
Brother: I want chocolate cookies.
Mother: You are allergic to chocolate cookies, and you must not eat any.
Hillary: Why is he allergic?
Mother: Because chocolate cookies are no good to eat, he gets sick.
Brother: I want to eat chocolate and I'm not sick.
Hillary: We pretend you are sick.
Mother: Yes.
Brother: I don't want to be sick.
Hillary: Well, you have to.
Brother: I won't play with you then.

Hillary: OK—You be the daddy and he is not sick.
Mother: I want to be the daddy.
Hillary: Well, we can only have one daddy.
Brother: I'm not hungry.

And off baby brother goes, leaving Hillary and the other little girl to play tea party, which they did in a very loud and aggressive fashion. Teacups were thrown around, cookies were spilled on the floor, and the tea party broke up when Hillary took all the dishes and put them into the pretend sink and said that they needed to be washed.

In this sequence of pretend play, the action follows as a consequence of the statements made by one child, and the other child's acceptance of these directions. At no time did the children set out to think about how the play would proceed. Instead, roles were given, directions accepted or rejected, and the interaction proceeded from one seemingly planned episode to another with little or no apparent thinking through of sequences. It appears that Hillary wanted the play to proceed and even offered alternatives for the baby brother. In this way she seemed to be thinking about ways to prolong the pretend play, but there was no evidence of an organized, well-developed cognitive structure within which these children were playing. Unlike Patrick's thought-through cake mixing, theirs was a spontaneous episode. Imagination is usually described as a way in which the young child will play out roles and discover for himself or herself what is involved in these roles. Often the definition of imagination includes the idea of exploring, for example, what mothers and fathers do, what teachers do, what the nurse or the plumber does. While it has been said that imagination imitates observed behaviour, this would seem to be a rather limiting definition, as often the play, artwork, drama or stories that we see as being most "imaginative" bear little resemblance to anything a young child has really seen.

We do not conceptualize imagination as finding out what a role *is*, but rather as thinking through what one *might do* in a particular role or situation. In this sense, when a child plays out a role, he or she utilizes pretend play, which forms the foundation from which the child will find out about what others do and what their role identities are. Perhaps as important to the child as finding out the activity content of roles is the discovery of how he or she *feels* when placed within such a role. The pretend play gives the child the ingredients that he or she can then "think with," so to speak. Patrick, for example, has no doubt pretended before to make a cake; he has probably watched and helped one of his parents to actually do so. In this way he has added the sequences and the materials necessary for the cake-making process to his thinking repertoire. It is then possible for him to imagine the cake-making process in his mind, verbalize parts of it, and, finally, to play it out in reality.

Imagination, we suggest, can best be described as the *thinking function* of pretend play; the imaginative thinking, which is the "what if" function, sets the stage for the actual activity of play, which is the "as if" activity. In other words, the thinking process is a higher order activity than the pretend play itself, although obviously the play is necessary in itself and facilitates further thinking and imagining processes. As a six-year-old said while manoeuvering his toy robot transformers, "You imagine in your head, and that tells you how to play"; imagining continues as the playing proceeds and becomes planning for further play action. It follows then that if the child does not have the opportunity of being involved in pretend play, imaginative thinking and the processes involved in that sort of thinking will be limited.

Pretend play, it seems to us, is a special category of play that involves a child's understanding and representation of reality. It is, in effect, a "what if/as if" situation. For example, the child thinks, "What if I were a fire fighter? What would I do?" The child thinks about this for a while, assembling the bits of reality known about fire fighters derived from story books, the comments of adults, observations of real life and television. The child first imagines what being a fire fighter would be like and how it would feel to be one, then plays it out "as if" he or she were one to the best of his or her ability, given the factual knowledge of the reality and the availability of props that can be used in the "as if" situation, the child says and does what he or she has imagined as fire fighter does. A group of three-year-olds I (Dr. Weininger) observed played out fire fighter roles with little variation. They made such comments as: the fire fighter "puts out fires," "saves people from high buildings," and "makes a lot of noise when he rides in the fire engine." But as they played these pretend roles, it became obvious that they stopped at times and seemed to be in the process of thinking. When I asked what they were thinking about, one of the three-year-olds said, "Firemen can save a cat when it's high up in a tree."

Dr. W.: What do you mean "high up in a tree"?

Terry: Well if a cat is so high up it can't get down then the fireman
          could climb his ladder and get the cat.
Dr. W.:   I think so. Why were you thinking about that?
Terry: Because cats climb up and firemen climb up.
Dr. W.:   So since they both climb, then maybe firemen could get a
          cat that's "high up in a tree"?
Terry: Yeah.
Dr. W.:   Did you ever see a cat high up in a tree and it couldn't get
          down?
Terry: No, but I just thought of it.

Terry seems to me to use his imaginative thinking processes to evolve
the idea of a cat that climbs and might need to be rescued by a fire fighter
who also climbs. Perhaps the ladders that these children were using in
their fire fighter pretend play gave Terry the concept of climbing, and
in his imagination he could visualize a cat climbing up and needing help to
get down again. Thus, pretend play provided the basis for the child's
further use of imaginative thinking. Although he did not go on to play
out this new possibility, we might reasonably expect to see an episode
with a cat show up at some time in the future when Terry plays fire
fighter or draws pictures of fire fighters and burning houses, which is the
activity with which he finished the morning's events here described.

Actual pretend play begins when a child uses a prop for something
other than the activity for which he or she has seen it used by a caregiver.
Thus, a hair brush becomes a sailing boat; a wooden block a hair brush;
or a stick a bridge. This usually happens when the child is about two
years old; that is when children seem to be capable of making an "as if"
transformation of an object, a necessary prerequisite to pretend play
involving objects, others, and himself "as if."

This recognition of the connection between imagining and pretending,
then imagining and pretending some more, has a special meaning for
adults who work with children who are ready to be involved in "what
if/as if"? It is very important for teachers of pre-school children to be
very good observers and listeners, to see what children play with, to
watch what they do with the materials, and to listen to what they say
about the props and materials provided to them. It is equally important
that the teacher becomes part of the play of the child, but—and this is
essential—at the developmental level that the child is showing. We all
remember the relative who insisted that the Fischer Price® garage could

only be a garage, not a part of the fortress wall; and the legendary behaviour of the father who gives the young child a gift of an electric train or racing car set and proceeds to insist that it be played with in terms of adult reality—it must represent the Grand Prix, we must stay with the same colour car, there can be no cheating by having one car fly over the other to win. The father ends up playing by himself as the child returns to the blocks where he or she is allowed to pretend without adult guidance and limitations.

The teacher should not be the leader or the organizer of the pretend play, and must try not form premature conclusions or make assumptions for the child. The teacher observes and asks questions about what the child says, and helps to draw information from the child, maintaining the conversation on the theme provided by the child, but at a pace which allows the child to feel comfortable and pleased with the conversation. The teacher also encourages children's play by providing props that extend the play but do not change the theme. In doing so, teachers provide for further pretend play and thereby a more effective basis from which thought processes and imagination can develop. Teachers help children with their thinking by making statements about their work— not evaluative statements such as "I like your cake," or assumptive ones, such as "What a naughty horse, eating up all the flowers"—but statements of the obvious on which the child can expand, such as "It's a high cake."

The following interlude is an example of how a teacher can encourage and facilitate without arranging or managing children's play. Two four-year-old girls wanted to play "pretending to go to the zoo," and had made pictures of the animals that they were going to see. The teacher suggested that they "might be able to use the blocks to make a special place for each of the animals in the zoo." The girls proceeded to make a rather elaborate setting for their picture animals, giving each one of them a separate space. When they had completed this work, the teacher asked if they needed some pieces of paper to make signs for the zoo. The girls readily used this, and to me it seemed like a very natural extension of their zoo play. They made pictures of the zoo animals on the small pieces of white cardboard and then pretended to write the names of the animals beside their pictures. They proudly showed their zoo to the teacher and any member of the class willing to come and visit. Then it occurred to one of the girls that they could charge admission when other children came to see the zoo, and this led to making money, making a map of the zoo, and, for one of them acting as a guide for the visitors. The pretend play spawned other pretend play activities, but all within the same "zoo theme"—and the teacher encouraged the children by suggesting ways only to extend it, not to change it; she recognized the richness of the play and helped them to develop it.

In pretend play, the children test out concepts, which are then added to their thinking repertoire and are available for a much higher level of reality testing, the testing out of concepts through interpersonal interactions and relationships. They begin to recognize that other children also behave according to their own "as if" constructions during pretend play; they start to see the need to be flexible, adaptable, and to be able to incorporate and integrate others' thinking and feeling into the play along with their own.

Another point of importance for the teacher of the young child is to recognize that the props and materials provided in the play area for children will be used in different ways, which give meaning and content to the pretend the children are currently involved in. Once a child is capable of "as if," the actual prop may seldom be used as it was intended. Thus a two-year-old may play with a spoon only as a utensil for eating, while a three-year-old may use it as a shovel or a bridge. Indeed, one three-and-a-half-year-old stated that it was "really an elevator" as he lifted the spoon from the floor to the chair, while a small fluffy dog sat on it! The materials might suggest to the child ideas for play, or imaginative connections that do not conform to the teacher's ideas for their use. This is the beginning of an important part of the problem solving process—the idea that the use for an object is contextual and not fixed for all time.

As children grow older, their capacity to make use of materials in relation to their fantasy increases. They begin to harness their fantasy in ways to help them understand their growing perceptions of the world about them. As they use materials to represent fantasy rather than reality objects and situations, they gradually begin to understand the concept of symbolism, which is really only the more adult version of the two-year-old's "as if" with a block for a boat. The five-year-old can say, and believe in the pretend play, "This paper cup is a magic cup that helps you fly when you're holding on to it." An understanding of symbolism would seem to underlie the development of thinking and understanding. If the child is not given the freedom and permission to use his or her imagination, then we may expect certain undesirable results. Exploration of symbolism may emerge much later than is expected—that is, after about four years of age—or worse, the child may remain at a concrete thinking level (Weininger, 1979).

Gradually the idea that "whatever I think will work" changes, as the child finds out that the play hypothesis he or she is working at has flaws or is not agreeable to the others involved. However, by this time she is nearly ready to change the almost totally egocentric nature of her behaviour in the pre-school years. The child has found out through pretend play that he doesn't know everything and may have to ask others for advice or information. But the child has also discovered that some of what he knows and imagines about the world is correct through play, and so has the confidence to ask questions without feeling like a "dummy."

Young children need adult interaction, not adult control; when they are permitted to control their play, to give it their own structure and to pace it at their own energy levels, then play is productive and fulfilling, and forms the basis for cognitive learning. However, this doesn't mean license; in addition to the freedom to explore, create and imagine with materials and props set out by the teacher, young children also need the safety provided by the teacher's understanding of the young child's needs for age-appropriate limits. Letting children play with clay doesn't mean the teacher has to be willing to let a four-year-old attach clay to the hair of every other child in the room without her interference!

Imagining—"what if"—is a solitary activity within the child's mind and is only sometimes overheard in actual words. Pretending—"as if"—is usually done with other children, or, for the child who has no one with whom to play, with imaginary people or dolls. The teacher is not there to force the process or to try to do the imagining or the pretending for children, although she has a vital function in the facilitation of both. The teacher guides, but does not control; questions, but does not judge; answers, but does not criticize. By so doing, the teacher fosters in the best possible ways the process of imagination, pretend play, and intellectual development in the children with whom he works.

PART THREE
PLAYING AND LANGUAGE LEARNING
ARE INDIVISIBLE

It has been said the human capacity for language is what sets us apart from all other animals. Although there are differences among the many of the estimated 5,500 languages spoken in the world, there are also many similarities. For instance, any language can be used to generate an almost infinite number of thoughts. Another important similarity is that children everywhere learn to speak the language that they hear around them, and they learn to reproduce it down to the finest detail.

The chapters that make up Part Three of this book (Chapters 8 to 10) address the sensitive issue of language learning which includes talking, reading, writing, spelling, and second language learning. Chapter 8 develops the theme of language as food for thought. Expanding on this analogy, the authors outline a series of questions which teachers should ask when developing a curriculum to promote optimal language development. Furthermore, the chapter examines how the social nature of play provides a natural environment for complex language use within the classroom setting. Chapter 9 opens up the "Pandora's Box" of second language learning for children. This chapter is divided into five parts each of which examines the topic from a different perspective. Part One looks at the topic of second language learning from both an historical and sociological perspective. Part Two attempts to identify the various issues and factors that must be taken into account when discussing second language learning. Part Three examines the assumptions on which early immersion learning is based. Part Four outlines the best methods for teaching children a second language. The final part discusses ways to deal with the problems that arise in immersion language learning for new immigrant children. Chapter 10 focuses on some of the problems associated with teaching children to read. In experiences, which are crucial before the child can formally learn to read.

Chapter 8

FOOD FOR THE MIND

Learning a language requires feeding the mind well, and that is a little bit like feeding the body well: both balance and variety are needed. A child seems to learn language best when he is offered a rich variety of possible experiences which provide for interaction and expression and, in particular, for play and dramatization. An adult who listens to a child with interest and sympathy and speaks with her in a manner which is both understandable and stimulating, like an adult who offers a child a variety of different foods and encourages her to sample many, is helping to nourish curiosity and a desire to experiment. A teacher of young children who is interested in promoting optimum language development should steer clear of verbal drills, flash cards, and formal correction of "errors." Rather the teacher should encourage a child to express her own ideas, give her a chance to repeat and consolidate verbal skills she already possesses, and, at the same time, expose her to appropriate stimulation which extends and enhances these skills.

Just as there are a wide variety of food preferences even in infancy, so there are widely differing styles of linguistic performance in early childhood, and all children will not react in the same way when they enter the classroom, even to the same environment and stimulation. A child from a home where a high degree of expressive freedom and complexity of verbal stimulation has been the norm will respond initially with more ease than a child used to speaking only when spoken to, and that in as direct and practical a manner as possible. Even the most "progressive" curriculum may to some extent pay unconscious tribute to the socioeconomic privilege which seems to be built into any educational system, unless the teacher takes special care to focus on individual children, and to recognize and make use of the varieties of language they bring with them to the classroom, their particular vulnerabilities and strengths.

To use the food analogy one more time, a teacher is unlikely to make fun of an unusual ethnic food which the child brings in her lunch bag, since she doesn't want to hurt the child's feelings or denigrate her cultural identity; but sometimes that same teacher might not recognize that the little girl's language patterns are just as clearly a part of that identity, and just as vulnerable to hurt.

The sort of flexible environment we have in mind will extend and enrich the linguistic awareness and capacities of children from various backgrounds by letting them interact in an informal manner, and by encouraging their different strengths to support each other. This is in contrast to the frequent reality of more conventional classrooms, which often manifestly reinforce the apparently 'superior' abilities of the advantaged child, the skills that smooth her so easily into the world of literacy and formal training, leaving the 'disadvantaged' child behind.

In order for the curriculum which evolves to make the most fruitful use of every appropriate resource and opportunity for the children's language development, the teacher has to ask a whole series of related questions in the planning stages.

First, about the children:

- Do they initiate conversations, or only respond to questions?
- Do they speak naturally with each other and/or the teacher?
- Do they work most frequently alone, together, or with the teacher?
- Are they able to handle the materials currently available?
- Are they all doing, generally, the same things?
- Do they seem to have special interests which they bring into the classroom?
- How do they seem to form strategies for learning?

Second, questions about the classroom and the adaptation of the children to it:

- Is the classroom a warm and comfortable place for the children?
- Does the day seem to be organized in a way which fits their needs for structure and for freedom?
- Does the organization of the classroom space allow for a variety of learning activities at the same time?
- Does the curriculum allow flexibility for individual programs and individual choices?
- Does the curriculum plan get discussed with the children themselves?
- Is the subject matter presented clearly and in a natural way?
- Are basic skills taught individually or in groups?

Third, questions about the responses of parents and colleagues:

- Do other adults find the classroom atmosphere welcoming?
- How does the principal think the children should be learning?

- Do the parents seem to demand early formal education?
- Do parents and colleagues understand the role of play and project in active learning?

Working from this information base, the teacher can mold a curriculum which encourages a good deal of verbal interaction of varying kinds. Perhaps the most important verbal technique the teacher can develop is a questioning style which permits her to listen sensitively to the children, and then to question them in ways which will stimulate and guide them, encouraging the use of language as a tool to describe and extend their cognitive functioning. She can avoid questions which demand convergent answers, "yes" and "no" responses, or press for a single "right" answer she has previously provided, as these don't allow a child time to feel her way towards what she wants to say or the freedom to answer in an unrestrained manner. By asking questions which help the child reveal her thinking to others—and, perhaps more importantly, to herself—through speech, the teacher is establishing a foundation for the child's emerging cognitive ability and for critical thinking.

For example, a teacher might ask, "What can you tell us about water?" and the children might respond, "It's wet and cold—but sometimes warm or even hot—it runs when you turn on the faucet—or the hose—and dogs and cats and people drink it—and flowers get watered by it—and firemen use it to put out fires—and we swim in it at the beach—or in a pool" and so on. There really is no "right" or "wrong" answer, and while listening to their responses, she is able to find out what they know about it before moving on to design a project which expands on their existing knowledge—perhaps about the displacement of water by objects. In preparation for this, she might begin to limit and order the responses, guiding the children toward more critical answers. So her next question, perhaps, would be "What else can you do with water?" which still allows for several answers but begins to focus the children's thoughts. Some might reply, "You can color it—you can paint with it—you can make kool aid with it—you can make ice with it".

Next the teacher might ask them "How do you know you can do these things?" Now she is asking for ways in which the children might explore or test these answers, setting up conditions for some simple experiments with water in the classroom. Perhaps the children will experiment with what things will colour water, or mix with it, and what happens when you put it in a freezer, or leave it out in the air for several days in a shallow pan in the sun, or put a large rock into it, then a larger sponge, then a block of wood. Later, she might ask "What did you find out from your experiments with water?" which suggests to them that they can evaluate what they saw and draw some conclusions. Through this kind of process she is helping them to develop critical and logical powers by dealing first with objects, then with the words which represent them, thus promoting the symbolic interplay between physical experience, language, and thought.

The children's sense of the uses of language might be further explored then by reversing the roles; the teacher might say, "What kind of questions would *you* like to ask *me* about water now?" Some children might ask the same sort of questions she had raised earlier, while others might invest them with new content or change their direction in various ways. The discussion might be concluded—for the moment anyway—by the teacher's asking," *Now* what do you think are important things about water?" This suggests that the children summarize what they have learned, and encourages them to focus the whole experience of finding out through questioning, discussing, and experimenting. Essentially this helps them to verbalize the mental concepts that they have been in the process of creating. (Sund, 1974; Macnamara, 1971)

A variety of academic skills, cognitive concepts, and moral and social ideas can be opened to young children in a natural way through this sort of questioning and listening which encourages children to freely explore as well as make use of their existing knowledge and resources. To use this technique effectively the teacher must obviously be very flexible and sensitive, yet at the same time capable of guiding the free discussion in the most profitable directions. Of course, she has to be really interested in what is happening in the classroom, not just going through the motions of a dialogue. She must focus on each child, give her time to think and speak, while simultaneously being alert to other children who want to help answer.

The aim should be genuine discussion, with the teacher encouraging the children to interact with each other, not simply one-to-one with her. By creating such a climate for discussion, where children and teacher alike can question the validity of statements and there is a continuous check on the accuracy of understanding, she helps them to evolve for themselves the ability to arrive at reasoned conclusions and to become aware of the pleasures and powers of language in the process.

We suspect that this kind of a classroom might also provide an invaluable opportunity for studying relationships between language and thought.

Such investigation might build from the base of the teacher's own need to develop methods of evaluating the children's progress in order to understand the potential of individual children and to identify difficulties and special talents. Perhaps, for example, rather than using conventional tests to evaluate cognitive, linguistic and social competencies, the teacher might find it more useful to keep a continuous learning log which registers changes in each child's responses, questions, and verbal interactions, as well as the specific character and content of such discussions. She might note the kinds of activities the child does, or proposes, and the degree of intricacy or creativity of language and thought which underlie them.

Such a log would be an invaluable empirical record of linguistic development in terms of the child's whole classroom experience. Although we recognize that this may be far too time-consuming for a teacher who has to organize the classroom and observe individuals within it at the same time, it might be a valuable tool for a student teacher, a teacher's aide, or a researcher working with the teacher to help understand the linkages between cognition and expression more thoroughly.

In addition to developing verbal techniques to enhance language development and empirical evaluation methods which reflect such developments effectively, the teacher needs to structure the classroom and the timetable to provide time for social play involving familiar materials. The classroom, for example, might have several different kinds of play areas, one of which is a "home center" which includes pots, dishes, cutlery, a teapot, a stove, a table and chairs, where children could organize "tea parties" or "family meals." In such circumstances children play with "grown up" activities, and thus with the vocabulary which fits them; the familiar situations and materials provide natural opportunities for the use of words which describe, compare, and classify.

Thus the teacher might draw attention to colours, using one colour cup with a different colour saucer, and trying to match colours with the teapot—or she might provide shelves in various materials—wood, metal, and plastic—and talk about putting one kind of dish on the wooden shelf, another on the plastic, and so forth. The children will probably respond by talking about the colours and materials of their things at home, which helps their ability to observe and recall details. Both the social situation and the real-life materials invite the kind of natural conversational interaction through which language develops.

More complex use of language can evolve naturally through play which draws upon a shared social situation outside the classroom. Thus the teacher might begin by telling a story about a Saturday morning visit to a grocery store, knowing that all the children are likely to have been to a similar store with their parents at one time or another. Having started the story, she encourages the children to add their details to it—what foods did they see, how were they arranged in different areas, what colours do they remember from the vegetables section—and then suggests that the children draw pictures of what they have seen and helps them to record the words which fit each picture. Essentially, she is encouraging the children to find the relationship between verbal skills and reading skills by making use of their intrinsic motivation and real life experiences.

Carried one step further, the children might make up stories about what MIGHT happen at a grocery store if they were to take a friendly dragon there, for example—and they might tell these, sharing and adding on to the fantasy, or put the story on as a play with dragon, vegetable and fruit masks, or make up a puppet play, or a dragon relay race with magic pass words to go with the movements. This sort of dramatic play becomes in turn a vehicle for further language development through the creative fantasy it invites. Throughout the whole process the children have become more aware, not only of the range of verbal skills, but also of the distinctions and relationships between fact and fiction.

Thus although the child's play is personal, through the tactfully directed play activities encouraged by the teacher, her language development enters the public domain—the realm of shared and communicable cognitive discovery and symbolic expression. For example, if the teacher helps the children make a stream and a road in the sand table, and encourages the use of small toys such as cars, trucks, lego blocks, and clay people, the children will quickly move to discussion. They will begin to talk of maps, directions, the stops, the hazards, places to build bridges, the buildings along the way, the people they see from their cars and what they're doing, where they're going; encouraged by the teacher they develop quite an extensive descriptive vocabulary.

Through this co-operative description process, and the additional information children will always add—about trips they have taken, and trains or buses or planes they have ridden in, and the cars they have at home, and the new building on the corner by their house—the teacher can help them extend their language skills without the introduction of unfamiliar materials or the scheduling of sightseeing trips outside the school (invariably chaotic and exhausting for the children, but especially for the teacher!)

Similarly, simple play with a large bucket of water will eventually lead to discoveries about the relationships between objects and words. If the teacher wishes to talk about floating and sinking, for example, she needs to bring in a variety of materials which do both, and to encourage exploration of the qualities of each material. The children will quickly take over and learn to sort and classify just about everything in the classroom as being "sinkable" and "floatable." Then the children can be encouraged to start a chart which uses symbols to describe which objects sink, and which float; in the same way, she can encourage the children to understand and relate words such as "heavy," "light," "rough," "smooth," "fluffy," "up," "down," "around," "behind," "underneath," "on top of," and so forth. In such a way they learn not only about the properties of objects in the natural world but also about the power of language to define and organize.

Clearly, the direction and model provided by the teacher in such a learning experience is important. At the same time, it is crucial that the play not be over-directed. The degree of intervention and the timing of the introduction of materials is obviously very important. If the play is interfered with too early, then it will cease or become less productive. If it is not encouraged or enriched by additional suggestions, it runs the risk of becoming boring, and the children will drift off to something else. To know how to pace the introduction of materials and how to choose the ones which will best exploit the potential for discovery created by the children's own activities is a very subtle skill which teachers must develop and refine for themselves through experience.

There is great potential for language development inherent in any and all of the classroom's materials and learning centres. Dialogue, questioning, storytelling, roleplaying, singing, fantasy development, word comprehension, vocabulary building—all these aspects of language use can be explored or emphasized in most classroom activities. The teacher must develop an acute sensitivity to the children's changing needs which allows her to act as a clear model for them, an active teacher of language, while at the same time ensuring their genuine participation in a learning experience which preserves the character of the very good early mother-child interactions.

To do so, she must not be impatient with the errors or idiosyncracies

of the child's language; she must give her sufficient opportunity to talk
without interruptions. The teacher must really listen to each child and
attempt to make sense of what she is saying. She must keep the dialogue
open by avoiding questions which invite a mere "yes" or "no," and by
resisting the impulse to correct or put words in the child's mouth. Of
course she uses correct language herself, not baby talk or current slang,
but she does not say what she wants the child to say. The modelling and
corrective force of the teacher's example works through such continuous
dialogue, just as it does in an effective parent-child model which influences each child's preschool language development.

From this basis of open dialogue and sensitive directive response to
the child's emerging capacities, such a classroom program naturally
extends to the full range of the pleasures of language—its formal complexities, aesthetic pleasures, and the ways in which it expands understanding of ourselves and the world. The formal conventions of written
language—standard English syntax, conventional spelling, punctuation,
capitalization, idiomatic usage—are introduced when the need for them
arises in a child's own attempts to represent his thinking in writing and
to read the writing of others. This will be a highly individualized
process, since decades of force-feeding such information to entire classes
at once, unconnected and irrelevant to their own written work, has
already shown us such non-individualized methods do not work.

Similarly, the child can be introduced to the nature of sound in her
language in a way which simultaneously ensures that her experience in
the classroom draws on her knowledge of the familiar world outside it.
The sounds which are part of the child's environment—her classroom,
her family home, the streets in her neighbourhood—can all be used as a
means of helping the child to attend closely to what goes on around her
and to begin to identify the sounds in terms of patterns and classes.
When the child is presented with a variety of sounds—machines, engines,
crying, laughing, typewriters, horns, instruments, ambulance sirens,
cars, trucks, thunder, rain, lightening, waterfalls—she listens, and sorts
sounds into categories, such as those made by machines, those made by
people which are not language, and natural sounds, and thus begins the
process of abstract thinking. Later, this capacity becomes more refined,
and the child can deal with sounds by talking about them as "high,"
"low," "soft," and "loud," and begins to see how she might recognize a
pattern in a sound to identify it by the next time she hears it.

This process is extended from these sounds to listening to and playing with the sounds of words—poetry, songs, jingles, jump rope chants—and re-combining them to make them rhyme, or be alliterative, or work in any other of the many ways we combine sounds to create an effect. Such listening activities help the child to organize the sounds, noises, and speech of her environment, and provide new imitational cues for words. And through listening to the child do this, the teacher is able to evaluate the child's ability for listening discrimination and for imitation of heard sounds. Can the child, for example, use consonants, recognize rhythm, use accurate intonation, and imitate the endings on words she has heard correctly?

Speaking with the other children, not just the teacher, is an essential part of a language program; the dialogue which goes on naturally in learning centres acts as one of the most effective mediums for the development of language. Within it, the children learn to use and understand the wide varieties of others' use of the language, outside their own family and cultural patterns. One child may say while playing, "Turn off the light and let the baby take a nap now", and another, checking out the meaning, may say, "Do you mean close the light and let the baby go to sleep?" In this manner they learn idiomatic phrasing and come to understand that there may be more than one way to say the same thing.

In a classroom atmosphere which values the individual child we can observe that the child's language is nurtured, enriched, refined, and expanded as her experience of herself and the world broadens. We would like to give one more example, a rather long one, of the way in which a teacher—a catalyst, a role model, a provider of resources, and a molder of opportunities which present themselves—operates to ensure that such an atmosphere is created.

In the "growing centre" the children watch while the teacher cuts carrots, and they sample them, and talk about the colour, the texture, and carrots from cans, frozen packages, in salads, and finally about carrots growing. The teacher explains that the leaves of the carrots grow out of their tops, and the children ask where the leaves have gone, and if it is possible to grow them again. So the teacher helps each child take a top of a carrot and put it in her own container of water, and as the days go by, they compare and contrast what is happening to each carrot top.

Some of the carrot tops grow, and the teacher talks about other things which grow from cuttings, like potatoes and onions, and about things which only grow from seeds, like beans. Next she brings in a variety of kinds of beans to taste and some to grow, and they watch as each bean grows in its own unique way, with leaves and perhaps flowers that are slightly different in colouring and in size. In watching and discussing what they see over time, the children learn to use taste, texture, size, and colour words as well as to understand on its simplest level how things grow, and how things may be the same in some ways and different in others. As they talk, the children learn to listen to the others, and to share their experiences—their family's garden, a visit to a farm, the flowers planted from last year's seed in a window box—and each learns to listen to herself questioning and refining her own ideas too.

The teacher extends the idea of growing things, but still within the realm of their known experiences, by talking about people growing up in families; perhaps she brings in clothes which might represent members of the family and people of different sizes and ages. Gradually the child gains a clearer understanding of the family unit and the differences and similarities among the people in it. Perhaps they each do a drawing of their 'family tree', and begin to understand the relationships between brother, sister, father, mother, grandparents, aunts, uncles, and cousins better as they do so. Sometimes the names given for the same connections are different, either culturally or through family habit—one child's "Pop-Pop" is another's "Zaidey"—and this allows the child to understand both the family's language as well as a more standardized form. The language of the family is of vital importance to a child, as her recognition of her place in the family tree is an essential part of her identity.

From the family tree, the development of the learning project may move to the family of man and to helping the children to gain an understanding of different people, different races, different cultures, different languages; like the variety of beans, they may be different but they are also the same. The teacher may read stories about different countries, and use pictures and objects the children bring from home, or slides, films, songs, and games in different languages. Perhaps the school can even invite parents from each ethnic group represented in the classroom to come in at special times and talk about being a child in the country where they grew up, and show or tell about what they wore and played with, what school was like, what holidays they celebrated, and teach a dance, a song, a poem, or even key words—"hello," "friend"—in their first language, and bring samples of a favourite food. Each parent helps the children to learn about different cultures in a joyful way, and such experiences help the children of each background to feel valued by the school, the teacher, and the other children. Perhaps each comes to see others' differences as interesting and attractive rather than as "weird" or "foreign." And all from a discussion about a carrot!

Language is food for thought; thought in turn prompts play, which leads again to language. Each link in this cyclical process between a child, her inner self, and the outer world is a vital part of cognitive, emotional, and psychological growth. Truly, then, we can think of the teacher as a careful cultivator of the classroom, a marvellous garden which can produce such food for the child's fertile mind.

Chapter 9

IN THE BEST OF ALL POSSIBLE WORLDS: SECOND LANGUAGE LEARNING FOR CHILDREN

An Historical and Sociological Overview of the Issues

Although generations of immigrant children in Canada have had to struggle to acquire either English or French as a second language, and far greater numbers have acquired a second and third language in the United States and Europe in the last two hundred years, it is only comparatively recently that a great deal of thought and effort has been spent in trying to understand the kinds of problems which arise in second language acquisition. Such an understanding is seen as central to finding more effective ways to teach a second language, both to new immigrants and to those within a society who wish to learn a second language widely used within the society.

Virtually simultaneously with the recognition of the need for this understanding, a variety of kinds of programs, variously labelled "immersion" (early, middle, or late) "structured immersion," "submersion," "bilingual immersion," "alternate immersion" and "heritage language" have been developed for the second language education of children. Because the programs have developed without necessarily having either a strong theoretical or practical, experiential base as an underpinning, in many cases it is only after several years of operation that research is being done to determine if, in fact, such programs accomplish what they set out to do. Proponents and opponents alike have tended to argue their positions from an emotional rather than an empirical point of view as a result.

This is largely because these programs are in response to a variety of "felt needs" within contemporary society, and thus they have goals which are philosophically, sociologically, politically, emotionally, and culturally influenced as well as being functions of the educational system. The diversity of programs, the rapidity with which they have been set up, the varying degrees of public acceptance with which they have been met, the curriculum materials and methods used, the skills of the teachers involved, and the heterogeneity or homogeneity of the populations

103

using them are all factors which must be considered in any evaluation of the effectiveness of such programs. A brief comparison of each of the "labels" above is necessary before the programs themselves can be considered with reference to these factors, however.

"Immersion," "structured immersion," and "submersion" language learning are simply different names for what is basically the same process. Early immersion is accomplished by ensuring that the four- or five-year-old child is prevented from using his or her first language during class sessions. The target language is used exclusively, and all verbal interactions, whether teacher-child, child-child, communal games, songs, or routine classroom instructions, and the study of all non-language subjects, like science, math, art, and physical education, are also conducted in this language. This continues at least for the first 3 or 4 years in school, at which time some subjects are usually taught in the child's first language, if maintenance of that language is considered as desirable. By this we mean that, for example, Mexican-American children or Chinese-Canadian children who are being immersed in English when Spanish or Chinese is their first language, will be expected to continue to study only in English, since the purpose of such a program is to make them fluent in English, whereas English speaking children who are in French Immersion programs to gain a second language within a generally English speaking community in Canada will eventually study at least English itself in English, as the intention is to make them bilingual.

"Middle" or "late immersion" refer basically to the same technique; the difference is in the age at which it begins. Mid-immersion tends to start at grade 4, late at 6. By this time, of course, students have been educated in a regular English curriculum, and they continue the study of English within the immersion French program. The degree to which other non-language studies are taught in French, English, or some blend of the two varies from program to program; generally the goal is that English only be used in subjects where it is assumed transfer of skills will not take place from one language to the next fast enough to ensure that no academic skills are weakened or lost in the process.

"Bilingual" or "alternate immersion" is more generally the pattern in the United States, where several hundred programs have sprung up since the 1974 Supreme Court decision (Lau vs. Nichols) mandated some form of bilingual education wherever it was needed. In such programs, the child's first language is maintained and used as a transition to the second, target language. As Ann Willig notes (1985), "since children receive instruction in their first language for a separate portion of the day, the continued development of first language skills and content learning is ensured. Any aspects of cognitive development that are dependent on language are able to evolve in a continuous fashion without the risk of a hiatus during the period of second language learning" (p. 308).

Such programs within the U.S. are almost entirely Hispanic, and many are carried out in communities where the dominant language is Spanish, in the home, in businesses, and in the media. Although almost certainly the intention is primarily to ensure that these children speak English fluently, these programs recognize that complete conversion to English as a first language for most of these children is unrealistic. There is an interesting parallel here to French Immersion programs run in the almost entirely English speaking milieu of southern Ontario; the goal in both cases is to develop students who are effectively bilingual although they may not get much chance to practise their new language within their own community. The irony is that most American programs, with the goal of turning an immigrant population into English speakers, recognize the importance of maintaining the first language in the classroom and in teaching non-language skills effectively in the early years, while most Canadian programs, with the goal of turning an English speaking population into a bilingual one, generally prefer the one-language-only approach. Variations in programming, however, occur year to year, and one must approach an individual school board if one wishes to know exactly how second language learning for children is being programmed.

In Canada a 50/50 program was developed by the Ottawa Roman Catholic Separate School Board in the 1970's, and evaluated at length in a review by Wilson and Connock (1982). The choice of such a model was predicated at least in part by the bilingual nature of the Ottawa area; the school population consisted of Catholic students who were Anglophones or Francophones, and it was presumed that each group should become bilingual without being split into two separate streams or schools. Thus children were mixed, regardless of first language, and studied in one language for half the day, and the other language for the other half, with two different teachers, each of whom was, if possible, a native speaker of the language in which she was teaching. An unusual feature of the population of this program was that, unlike most large urban areas in Canada, fewer than 6% of the students reported themselves as speaking a third language, other than French or English, before they came to school. By contrast, nearly 60% of the population of Toronto speaks a language other than either French or English at home.

"Heritage language" programs are a newer arrival on the language teaching scene in Canada; the term means, basically, that the school system will attempt to help students whose first language is neither English nor French to maintain it, in the face of immersion in English in the regular classroom for new immigrant children, and the addition of French classes to their linguistic load later in the school program. It tends to operate only in the larger urban areas with a wide range of first languages, and then on a "demand" basis. In other words, according to Ontario Ministry of Education criteria, if a certain minimum number of parents request a heritage language program in their neighborhood school, or if a school system wishes to provide it within the framework of the regular school day, the ministry will give financial support. Thus each school board basically determines when and where such classes will be held. These classes are meant not only to allow children to maintain their first language, but to absorb the culture of that country as well, and, emotionally, to be assured that the school, and by extension the society, values them and the culture from which they spring.

As one might imagine, this can create difficulties. In a school which is required to offer classes in Chinese, Greek, Russian, Hebrew, Spanish, Portuguese, and Italian (not unusual in Toronto), finding teachers who are competent to teach each language is difficult; more difficult yet is to know what to do with the kids who are "none of the above" during the period in which heritage language programs are being taught. Legally any child may enroll in a heritage language program operated in his school, regardless of whether he speaks that language, but this has not widely been utilized. What has happened, in such cases, is that the school day has been lengthened, and non-teachers brought in to teach heritage language classes during the middle of the day, providing the regular classroom teachers with a break; students who do not participate are "occupied" by teacher's aides.

It is doubtful whether even the strongest supporters of heritage language programs would argue that they teach a second language, although they may act psychologically to keep children from discarding their first language, and thus cutting themselves off in some ways from their families' language and culture. And critics of such programs, like critics of many of the bilingual or alternate programs in the United States, argue that it is the job of the school to integrate newcomers as quickly as possible into their new country, and that allowing, or encouraging, students to maintain a first language hinders assimilation into the mainstream language and culture.

The heritage language program is, however, an attempt to come to grips with one of the realities of a country which is multi- rather than bilingual. Although this is a widespread problem in Canada, until relatively recently, it has not been in the U.S., where the existing population is made up of largely third or fourth generation immigrants from European countries who arrived in the great migratory period of American history, which ended prior to the first world war. Additional refugees arrived after the second world war, but most came to established "hyphenated" ethnic communities and assimilated quickly. The exceptions to this are the large number of refugees from Indochina who have arrived in the last decade, and the increasing numbers of Spanish speaking peoples arriving from the economic and political chaos of Mexico, Central, and South America. Thus the problem for most American schools continues to be dealing with a relatively small number of different languages, with a relatively high geographical concentration of Spanish, at least, in the southwest.

In Canada, however, the problem is somewhat more complicated; we shall, for most of this chapter, use the current Canadian reality as our primary focus, as we are most familiar with it. It is a key educational and political issue at present in Canada, where both French and English have equal historical status as "first languages." Far more people speak English than French outside of Quebec, although most provinces have pockets of French majority communities. Federal government policy mandates most services and signs in both languages outside Quebec, but inside Quebec, the policy is adamantly Francophone only. Signs are not allowed in English on the outsides of stores, for example, and Quebec natives are not-so-subtly encouraged to remain monolingual, in spite of the influences of both the United States and the rest of Canada toward English as the "lingua franca" of the continent.

Immigrant children coming to Quebec are not allowed to attend schools in the English stream unless their parents come from an English speaking country; a family arriving from Italy, for example, must educate their children in the French stream whether they want to or not, thus ensuring that their children will be French and Italian speaking, but that they will have difficulty in learning English well enough, at least at school, to operate easily in the rest of the country. Francophones perceive all these measures as being essential to the continued existence of the French language and culture in Canada; bilingualism is not seen by most of them as either emotionally or culturally positive, but rather as an unfortunately unavoidable economic reality for those involved in national or international business or tourism.

This has, predictably, created a strong emotional backlash in some parts of the country which are virtually monolingually English, or which have large numbers of people who speak any one of the more than 50 other languages spoken in Canada. They see as blatantly unfair a system which requires their children to learn French, provincial governments which push everyone toward becoming officially bilingual, and civil service jobs even in non-French speaking areas as requiring fluency in French, while Quebec is allowed to be aggressively non-English in policy and practice.

The paradox is that regardless of the exodus from Quebec over the last ten years of people who want their children educated in English, or at any rate not *only* in French, and who see jobs in Quebec decreasing for those who are not fluently French speaking, Immersion French schooling is seen by many upper middle class English speaking families outside Quebec as an essential social and economic goal—and in some cases, a status symbol. In many communities a third language is far more prevalent in homes and businesses than either English or French, and realistically, that language would be far more useful for English speaking children to acquire than is French in terms of career opportunities and community solidarity.

Isaac Bar-Lewaw, a professor of linguistics at York University in Toronto who speaks 12 languages himself, was quoted by the Toronto Star in an article on French Immersion (Zarzour, 1986) as saying that few French Immersion graduates will ever use or practise their second language, and that such programs are just expensive fads which will not make the country bilingual. "Toronto children need Italian more than they need French, and kids in Vancouver need to know Chinese and Japanese, and in Saskatoon they need to know Ukranian. But you could be completely bilingual in Toronto and never use the language," he concluded.

Most young children who go to school in North America will pick up English—in the classrooms, on the streets, from TV and radio—relatively quickly, and progress on to study in other disciplines with at least some degree of competency. And most students in schools in Ontario and most of the other provinces will pick up enough French in the required "core" classes (in Ontario, twenty minutes a day beginning at least by grade seven and continuing through a full credit grade nine high school course) so that if they really desire to become bilingual they will have the basis on which to build in high school or university courses, or through travel or classes in adult life.

Although we realize the heretical nature of this statement, we will nonetheless voice it: anyone, child or adult, who really wants to learn French can do so at any age, in or out of the school system. In the final analysis, if families really desire bilingual children in Canada, they can always move to Quebec, or send their children on an exchange to Quebec, France, or Switzerland, and thus accomplish it with far less hassle and expense for the society at large. It is a luxury, albeit a nicely nationalistic one, not a necessity in most areas of Canada today. As a corollary, the vast majority of the money now being spent for French Immersion classes might far better be directed toward achieving fluency in English for new immigrants to Canada (or in French, for those immigrating to Quebec.) Not only does their personal economic and social integration into society depend on it, but the country as a whole has a far greater need for adults who are literate and productive in English than it does for a handful of middle class bilingual children who may or may not ever use—or need to use—French.

This devil's advocate position aside, we can summarize by saying that, at least in some sections of Canada, the general assumption is that a bilingual population will contribute to the cultural wealth and political health of the country, and many middle class parents of English speaking children see their fluency in French as helpful in the job market and as a bonus, culturally or socially, in adulthood. It is also assumed that new immigrants will learn not only English, but also in most cases French in the schools, but that retaining some kind of emotional connection to their original culture and language is to be tolerated if not necessarily encouraged. In the United States the assumption is made that continued and rapid assimilation of new immigrants into the mainstream culture is economically and culturally desirable, and that fluency in English is essential to this goal; there are not, of course, the same historical reasons for maintaining a universal second language as are present in Canada.

Identification of the Crucial Issues for Discussion

From this very brief introduction to a very complex linguistic and political situation, it can be seen that a wide variety of issues and factors must be taken into account when discussing second language learning today. There are several major questions which must be posed in light of the above:

- what educational method(s) will best achieve French/English bilingualism for those who desire it in Canada, while ensuring equally strong skills in the first language and in other academic areas?
- what educational method(s) will best achieve fluency in a second language for students from a wide variety of linguistic backgrounds, while retaining their cultural and personal self esteem?
- what educational method(s) will best achieve fluency in a second language within a milieu where most, or all, of the children speak the same first language at home and in the community?
- what educational method(s) will best achieve fluency in a second language without sacrificing first language learning, and academic competencies established in that language, particularly for adolescents or adults entering the school system?

Clearly, a thorough investigation of all of these would require far more than a single article, study or book. The third is perhaps best addressed by those working in the field in the United States, and the fourth is an issue we would like to research and write about in greater depth at a later time, particularly in light of emerging knowledge about language learning and interhemispheric specialization. We will, therefore, focus on the first two, which are, in some ways, opposite sides of the same emotional coin.

The Rationale for Early Immersion Learning

The rationale for early immersion second language learning seems to be based on three assumptions:

First, it is to take advantage of the so called "fast acquisition" stage of children's linguistic development—the stage during which the child is best able to acquire fluency in any language, given suitable and adequate input. This is seen to be still sufficiently operational in children at the age of four.

Second, the child's brain at this age is still in a state of considerable plasticity, as evidenced by recovery from brain damage during the early years. This evidence is taken to suggest that language is not strongly lateralized within one hemisphere of the infant's brain. This, in turn, is interpreted as indicating a greater "malleability" allowing for the brain to cope with the separate linguistic inputs in much the same way as it appears to use different areas of the brain when compensating for damaged functions.

And third, the child is said to acquire a better accent and greater self-confidence in the target language if he is immersed at this early age.

In theory, all of these notions make very good sense; but there is growing evidence that one should be very conservative in accepting the assumptions made, as there are many factors which must be taken into account. Some of these should be of special concern to teachers and to parents of children who are being considered for entry into these programs.

As it is a lesser issue, let us first consider the argument for "better accent/ greater self confidence." How does one measure what is "better" accent, in any language? Native speakers of any tongue show regional accents which are often very different, even though they all understand each other. It is usually the socio-economically advantaged, or those from culturally-prestigious areas, who set the standards for "pure" articulation, which then becomes the "stuff" of elocution classes. What this means, of course, is that the child who is learning, say, French, will be taught the accent considered to be that of the more advantaged of French nationals or of those who speak "Parisian" French. People vary in the degree to which they can mimic precisely what they hear, so there is always a range of accents produced, not only in small children, but also in the teachers.

Surely, fluency in a language is the best determinant of how much the speaker will be understood, and how confident he will feel to speak it, given that he produces a fair facsimile of the required pronunciation? In Canada, especially, tolerance of a diversity of accents is a way of life and in no way detracts from verbal interactions and mutual understandings, given fluency in the language. It is also the case that intensive and meticulous training in pronunciation can make even adults improve their accents, so it may be a matter of teaching methods, rather than student abilities, which determines the quality to at least some degree. It is therefore suggested that the "better accent" factor is not sufficient rationale for immersion programs.

Confidence in one's speaking ability is most generally acquired by regular oral work—in any language, those who speak aloud, in front of or to others, most frequently are the most confident and relaxed public speakers. Certainly knowing a language well makes one more willing to try to conduct conversations in it, but opportunity to do so in a natural way is just as important. Many students of foreign languages at all ages become quite adept at translating and grammar, but are seldom in out-of-class situations where real conversations happen, and thus acquire neither fluency nor confidence in their oral language skills.

One of the most thorough studies done of methods in use in immersion classrooms, JK-6 is that done by Ireland, Gunnell, & Santerre (1981), and the criticisms they make include the apparent non-integration of formal and functional teaching situations. That is, the sense that too often there is little apparent relationship between formal language instruction, which teaches some aspect of the language structure or grammar regardless of the utility of the examples used, and functional situations, in which the language learning is only incidental to the subject matter content. Other criticisms they have are that too often the teacher talks more than all the students put together, which increases listening skills but doesn't allow much practice in speaking; the teacher is too often the only one to give directions, explain, describe, request or ask questions, which keeps students from practising most key language functions; teachers' questions are often answerable with very short answers, which they often elaborate on or reformulate rather than encouraging students to do so; and teachers do not share opportunities with the students for speaking. In addition, not enough of the content is relevant enough to students' lives to encourage them to converse between themselves outside of school, in a more informal manner, and there is often little chance for practise within the community or family which increases oral fluency and confidence. This same comment, of course, can be made about the general methods by which many subjects are taught in any school, English or French speaking.

If the goal is to increase oral fluency, then, it is possible that immersion programs are too artificial (too "schoolish") by their very nature to do so, at least when the students being immersed are from families and/or a community in which the target language is not frequently spoken. This is in contrast to the experience of many immigrant children immersed in English not only in the school but on the playgrounds, in the stores, and from the media; such children frequently comment that they learned more English, and much faster, from TV and playing with English speaking children than they did in school!

The other two reasons given to justify immersion programs for four-year-olds, that of using the "fast acquisition" stage, and taking advantage at the same time of the child's cortical plasticity, are much more complex issues. They imply that the child, by virtue of being immersed in the target language in this way, is being placed in a "natural" condition for its acquisition. The question then arises—is this really so? Does the immersion program present the target language in a manner analogous to natural acquisition?

At base is the question of whether or not a child does *acquire* language, or whether it is taught in all cases. Most arguments around this issue degenerate into exercises in semantics, but Krashen (in Ritchie, 1978) suggests that *acquisition*, in the sense that no formal teaching is involved, is the means by which the child learns what "sounds right" in his language through daily exposure to his environment. He considers *learning* a matter of being taught linguistic rules through formal teaching methods. The ability to form mental representations of these rules then allows for more formal speech, as generally used in reading and writing. Krashen also argues that natural environments do not introduce the rules of grammar, syntax, and so on, one at a time, while providing feedback and error correction, as does formal teaching.

One could argue that the child who realizes a rule, such as -ed for past tense, overgeneralizes it, differentiates the exceptions and corrects himself as he matches his output with environmental input, is learning one rule at a time while using feedback and error correction, but without formal teaching. This, then, would imply that formal teaching and environmental linguistic experience are, in effect, the same thing, but this is not so. What formal teaching does is teach the child how the language should be used—the environment teaches how it is used within a particular social group. These two can be so different that even a child who has always spoken English can enter an English-speaking school to find himself confused by "school English," as opposed to "home English" (Gibson & Levin, 1975). The immersion program, then, is formal teaching. It may not specifically explain the concepts of rules to the child, but it teaches the language as it should be used, and follows a set curriculum.

One must also ask: IS the four-year-old in "fast acquisition" stage of language? Most of the literature appears to suggest that proficient language skill is acquired in a very short span of time, emerging, as it were, full-blown, somewhat similar to the manner in which a butterfly emerges from its chrysalis. This is an oversimplified picture of the process of linguistic cognition.

The assumption that language is innate, with all of it contained within the child's *competence*, although taking time to develop optimal *performance* (Chomsky, 1972), overlooks the fact that the linguistic complex—the hearing, speaking, reading, writing and making meaning of language—is organized within the highest cortical levels (Luria, 1966; Hecaen & Albert, 1978). When a child is born, this part of his cerebral cortex is not operational; but through growth and with the aid of adequate stimulation it develops the necessary neuronal activity and functional linkages which allow for systematic cognitive growth. There is a sequential maturation of the various portions of these higher levels, in terms of their functional strength and integration. (Whitaker, 1978; Luria, 1966; Yakolev & Lecours, 1967).

As this development occurs, environmental input stimulates and effects development and programming of appropriate cortical areas. The reason the baby does not speak is that his cortical language-processing system is not yet operational. However, the child who hears language as his language centres are developing, who tries to repeat it and then corrects himself as he receives his own and environmental feedback, will at the same time develop the language centres still more. He is laying down the neuronal firing patterns which become automatized and habitually available in the highest levels of his brain.

In all discussions concerning language, the levels of acquisition are measured by the child's speech production. Although it is recognized that children learn to understand verbal input before they can produce it, very few researchers have considered the fact that children hear speech long before they produce it. By six months old, his babbling might suggest the speech sounds and intonations of the environmental input, but the child is not expected to speak (Dale, 1976). Infants use intonation, gesture, manipulation of objects and many other strategies to make themselves understood and to develop their understanding of language, all the while building up their linguistic hierarchy from the simple to the complex. They learn to differentiate the speech sounds and to make the articulatory movements by constantly monitoring their own performance against that of others. Speech-sound differentiation is highly specialized; the analysis of phonemes, as opposed to non-speech sounds, has been specially noted as an essential prerequisite to the speech process by neuropsychologists (Luria, 1966; Maruszewski, 1975). As the complexity of the child's linguistic repertoire develops, so does the complexity of his neurological activity and integration within the higher cortical zones (Luria, 1966).

By the time the young child is producing complex sentences and taking part in discourse, he has not suddenly acquired language—he has merely reached the point where his cortical functional systems have evolved into the integrative complexity which allows this to happen. By four years old, this has already taken place to an astonishing degree, but it has taken four years to do so. From here on, he can construct his language and develop his verbal thought at the same time, but he does so by using language which has concrete meaning for him and which has reference to his immediate life. He learns by recognizing differences—a method of refinement which leads to more precise organization of categories of meaning (Ervin-Tripp, in von Raffler-Engel and Lebrun, 1976).

One researcher, at least, appears to suggest that children should learn their second language in the same manner as they learned their first—listening, parroting sounds, going through the telegraphic style of speech, and so on (Anderson, in Ritchie, 1978). Although this would appear to be a very sensible suggestion, given the known behaviour of the brain in setting up functional systems, no studies appear to have addressed themselves to the issue, for either children or adults.

However, there have been studies which support the hypothesis that the sounds of the language must be assimilated, at least to some degree, before they can be articulated (Gary, in Ritchie, 1978). Learners of a second language were not required to produce words, unless they wished to, but were given up to three months in which to assimilate to the sounds of the input. They were given exercises in which they indicated their understanding non-verbally, on the hypothesis that they needed to understand how the language was constructed (how it "had to sound"), before trying to construct it for themselves. This study, done with adults, followed on the observation that children comprehend sentences at least six months before speaking; and thus, requiring them to speak the second language while trying to process the unfamiliar sounds and relating them to their meaning might interfere with learning. This would then prevent long term storage of the language, to some extent, so that less would be available for recall.

Gary (1978) also pointed out that speaking is the *result*, not the *cause*, of language learning, as was noted above. It is obvious that a period of just listening to language before speaking it is more consistent with the manner in which children initially acquire their language skill. It may well be that failure to allow students time for the various sounds to become familiar and organized within the cortex before they are required to produce them is one of the most important "sins of omission" in second language classrooms for any age group.

There is still, however, a good deal which we don't yet understand about children's acquisition of meaning and understanding. We need to develop a coordinated use of observational and experimental methodologies to enhance our knowledge of language acquisition (Wells, 1982). For example, Wells points out in an earlier study that we don't know how to measure language development successfully, nor do we have any reliable instruments for educational communicative assessments: we need, he says, to "understand a great deal more about how we are able to carry on a conversation at all." (Wells, 1978, p. 467) Given the complexity of the relationship of first language acquisition to second language learning, we need to develop a variety of models for gradual exploitation of children's language and learning resources, involving an exploration of the values and limitations of code switching (Weininger, 1981) and emphasis on activity based learning.

When presented with a second language within the early immersion program, the child does not have the opportunity to follow the most natural sequence of development, but it is nonetheless assumed he will absorb the new language without difficulty. This overlooks the fact that all learning must follow the necessary processing which develops those neurological correlates which store the information for continual use. At the same time, the four-year-old's language skills are still not highly developed or highly habituated, in neurological terms, and so do not have the same degree of resistance to interference that can be expected at a later age (Luria, 1966). So, if a child is not already well habituated to a word in association with its meaning in his first language—say, for instance, that he had only once heard the word "dog"—then being presented with "chien" and toy dog many times in class may make it difficult for him to produce the English word, because the French one would take precedence in his developing language centres, and be automatically produced when he sees a dog. The child does not have more than one language-processing system in the brain—whatever he puts into it most frequently will be the material which is most easily retrieved.

One might well ask—what about those children who acquire two languages at once? There are many children who are exposed to two languages from birth and appear to acquire each language equally well. This is so, but it has been found that they develop each language in the same manner, to the same degree, but at a slower rate than one would expect for monolingual development (Hoffer, in von Raffler-Engel and Lebrun, 1976). It has been suggested that this is because they are learning twice as much while assimilating the differences between the two languages. It is also the case that the developing cortical areas involved have only the capacity which is available at any particular stage, so that coping with two languages means that each one has less neurological "space" available, because it is "shared." That this may be the case is strongly suggested by one study of adults who were bilingual (Ojemann & Whitaker, 1978).

In any case, the acquisition of two languages in this manner, where the differences are being analysed and assimilated from birth, is a very different process from that of putting a child in an immersion class when he has already been acquiring his first language for four years. The child has been learning language in association with objects, happenings and sensations which he has experienced repeatedly in his life, so that he uses words, according to the sophistication of his language, in association with his understanding of their meaning. That language changes in relation to the acquisition of more precise understanding of meaning was pointed out many years ago (Vygotsky, 1962). The small child does not name unfamiliar objects—he must first find out what the object is and then learn the name for it. The small child has literally to "sense" his way around his world, in all meanings of the word, building up his categories of meaning as he goes. Parroting songs and playing games may give very good training in articulation, but does not appear to guarantee that the child will assimilate meaning which can be applied in other situations.

In contrast, the adolescent who has mastered language to the adult level has an advantage in that he can apply his stored verbal meanings to incoming information (Luria, 1976). Also, many studies have indicated that older learners acquire the cognitive and academic components of a second language faster than do younger students, although there seems to be little difference in terms of their ability to develop strong oral skills (Cummins, Swain, Nakajuma, Handscombe, Green & Tran, 1982b). And as Hakuta (1986) rather reluctantly points out, there is substantial evidence to suggest that adolescents learn second languages more quickly and more effectively than do younger children; only in the acquiring of phonology is there no difference between the two. Our "gut" sense that the earlier one is exposed to a second language, the easier it will be to learn, and the more fluent the speaker will be, may be based on informal comparisons of children who have been immersed in an alien environment contrasted with older people who have only received instruction in school (Gardner, 1986).

An alternative model for immersion based on more accurately meeting the needs of young children for experientially based, gradual acquisition without the necessity for immediate production, was, quite interestingly, developed in Wales as early as 1967. It proposed a program which advanced in stages; during the initial stage the child was simply exposed to the teacher's language in situations clearly related to the child's activities, and any response which involved both comprehension and communication, in either language, was accepted. In the next stage, the child acquired passive learning of language concepts related to his daily experiences through hearing them repeated in appropriate contexts; only in the third and last stage was the child expected to actively use the second language. This program seems to be a particularly exciting one, however, no contemporary models of it seem to be officially recorded in Canada or the U.S. (Morgan, 1984).

It is essential that educators also become aware of the manner in which children process information, as well as the way in which the brain matures and organizes itself in relation to both age and environmental input. Nowhere is this more imperative than in the teaching of languages. In studies of lateralization of language, it is usually the case that "language" and "speech" are treated as if they were basic functions. This is not so, as has been clearly demonstrated in neuropsychology (Luria, 1966; Konorski, 1967; Hecaen & Albert, 1978). Any of the language skills result from the interaction and harmonizing of many different basic functions which can be exclusive to that particular skill, but might also be part of many other skills. One of these is sequential-ordering of sound, which is a function of the temporal lobe of the dominant hemisphere. For refined analysis of language, whether reception or expression, the ability to automatically keep the phonemes in order, so that words are understood, processed, and articulated in a precise manner, is all-important (Luria, 1966).

We know that the 4-year-old has already managed to organize his sequences of sound into good receptive and expressive language skills, so it would seem that this would be a good age to start acquiring a second language. And it can be argued that early immersion classes have been shown to be an effective, natural, and potentially enriching experience in many cases, irrespective of the role research in neurological development may play in their planning. This is not surprising, if one really looks at what is going on. The 4-year-old is placed within the formal class setting and then given holistic input of language—whole words, sentences, and so on—but at the level of language which is normal for a child of his age. Simple, concrete sentences and simple songs can be processed in a "Gestalt" manner, which is the function of the non-dominant hemisphere of the brain. In the very young child, this type of processing is at least as efficient, and usually more so, than the analytical processing which is the function of the dominant hemisphere.

Clearly, given optimal circumstances, early immersion is not only an efficient, but perhaps the only, method which will ensure rapid second language learning in a school setting. As Cummins says, "countless evaluations from all across Canada have consistently shown that students in [early French immersion] achieve high levels of French proficiency at no apparent academic cost" (1982, p. 42). The transfer of academic skills which occurs at the switch from one language to the other will be effective, he suggests, providing the student is adequately exposed to the majority language and has the motivation to learn it.

At the same time, such students may reap "cognitive advantages associated with attaining an additive form of early bilingualism" (Cummins, 1978), in the form not only of enhanced English language skills but also in specific intellectual skills due to the increased metalinguistic awareness raised by their experiences in the immersion process (Swain & Lapkin, 1981). Of course, one might question whether this evidence simply emphasizes the relationship between cognitive ability and linguistic skills which made such students optimal candidates for immersion to start out with, rather than the possible effects of early immersion *per se.*

Moreover, early immersion may not be laying down the processing linkages and functional systems which lead to the complex and automatic analysis and synthesis which are necessary for the mature development and use of language (Luria, 1966; 1970). Early immersion programs, then, may not give the child the most efficient "basic tools" with which to carry out the highly complex job of learning and using language. Moreover, to immerse the child in a "whole" language which is totally strange, and for which his brain is not programmed to cope, is as traumatic as it would be to put him on skis for the first time in his life and expect him to manage the slopes of Squaw Valley. He may stay on his feet, he may even survive to become a great skier, but only when he has overcome the initial fear and shock. The child who finds himself suddenly cut off from communication because he cannot use the language in which, at 4 years old, he is just becoming proficient, at the same time as he is expected to converse in a strange and totally unintelligible tongue, goes through a similar experience.

In addition, early immersion classes do not take into account the development of the child's brain, in terms of the maturation of the areas involved in particular processes. In Piagetian terms, concrete operations, the processes by which the child performs logical operations and begins to form classes and understand relations, begin at about 7 years old. It has been shown that a relationship between language and operational levels can be demonstrated (Sinclair, cited in Kessler, 1971). It has also been suggested that the child who is not yet at this stage does not understand two languages as separate entities, but develops awareness of their differences as he matures and develops a more abstract mode of thought (Kessler, 1971).

A central problem in assessing accurately the impact of various starting points in immersion language learning, or of various models, is, as Willig (1986) points out in her conclusion, the generally weak quality of research and evaluation in bilingual education. Of some 300 studies, for instance, Baker and deKanter (1981) found that only 28 met their criteria for methodological adequacy. Inadequacies typically exist in research design, failure to describe programs being examined, poor statistical treatment of data, and failure to equate the experimental and comparison groups on such characteristics as language proficiency and socioeconomic status.

Comparisons of fluency in English or other academic areas between French Immersion students and non-immersion students, even within the same school system, are difficult because immersion populations are self-selected and tend to be rather homogeneous in terms of ethnic origin and socio-economic levels. The perception of many non-immersion teachers and parents is that such programs are elitist and tend to segregate the children of largely Anglosaxon professionals from other ethnic groups, new immigrants, and working class families. One large Toronto area board has eight immersion programs in operation, and all but one are in up-scale neighborhoods; a casual glance at the populations of these programs shows a far smaller number of students from visible minorities than one generally finds in Toronto's increasingly multicultural milieu.

In addition, parents do not tend to place children who might have trouble with the additional stresses of immersion classes into them; in most boards parents can have either immersion or special education help, but not both at the same time, so there are relatively few learning disabled, academically slow, or emotionally disturbed children in them. Children who do have trouble tend to drop out into the English stream, where remedial help is more likely to be available, leaving a rather academically elite population as well. A Toronto Star article stated that up to 50% of French Immersion students leave the program by grade 8, in spite of the degree to which students are such an academically elite group.

The dearth of solid research contributes, then, to the rather polarized debates about immersion schooling in Canada. Adding to the dissension about the linguistic effectiveness of such classes are the social and economic complications: over 75,000 students are in immersion programs in Ontario alone (Zarzour, 1986) for example, and in some schools burgeoning French programs force busing of neighborhood children to English speaking programs elsewhere, which is very divisive. And there are far higher costs for immersion—the Etobicoke board, in the Metro Toronto area, estimated that it cost an additional $6,000 in textbooks and library materials to start up an immersion class, in addition to about $1,000 to bus each student. Retraining teachers to be fluent enough to teach in immersion programming is costly in both time and money; the Toronto board set aside $400,000 for this purpose from 1985–88, and North York estimates the cost of retraining at York University's bilingual Glendon College at $20,000 per teacher (Zarzour, 1986).

Cummins (1982) believes that in spite of economic and social factors such as these, and such research problems as Willig (1986) and others have cited, it can reliably be concluded that early immersion as it exists in most schools in Canada today is achieving its major goals well. He goes on to state that researchers have found that middle and late immersion achieve these objectives just as well as early immersion, citing the findings of Genesee (1978–79) as one example (see also McLaughlin, 1981, and Snow, 1981). If later second language learning can be at least as efficient, it could be argued that an innovative first language program, followed by such later, intensive immersion, might achieve the same or better results.

It seems logical to suggest that children, from the age of about seven onwards, appear to reach and pass many cognitive milestones. By this time, the child's first language is well established and he is already learning the grammar, syntax, and so on, which teach him how to understand his own language, as well as any other he may learn (Krashen, in Ritchie, 1978). His frontal lobes are "very young," in terms of their setting up of functional linkages, so might be expected to be working in the "fast acquisition" manner which appears to accompany other areas as they initially become established.

This means the child of 7 to 9 years old might be better equipped to learn a second language than she has been at any time before that age, given that it is not a language to which she has been constantly exposed since birth. As it is established that children lose a great deal of their cortical plasticity by the age of 10 or 11 years, second language instruction ideally should at least begin by this age. It may well be that such children would be able to reach a fluency equal to or surpassing children of the same age who have been immersed at four, by the time both groups reach puberty.

Optimal Methods for Second Language Teaching

The methods by which children might most effectively be taught a second language should be discussed logically in the light of the above information. Let us consider first the English-speaking child who must learn French as a curriculum requirement. By the age of 7 or so, according to intelligence and experience, he has a command of English which is, in all basic aspects, similar to that of an adult and all of his higher cortical processing areas in operation. As has been noted above, he must first *hear* the language and become conversant with its sounds. This should be within the context of experiences which relate to his daily life, for which he has already assimilated meaning.

The child should respond either in *English,* in this case, or non-verbally. In responding in her first language, the child is showing that she understands the meaning of what is being said to her and she is beginning to understand the differences between her own and the target language. The classroom should be a place in which the child can converse in this manner while enjoying various kinds of activities which relate to her everyday life, so that the language becomes a practical tool. This is certainly one of the goals of current early immersion teaching, although the degree to which it has been achieved has been questioned by Ireland et al., (1981), among others.

The child should be encouraged to respond in the target language whenever he feels he is ready to do so, and to the extent that he wishes. Fear of making mistakes might keep a child mute in the target language, but that does not necessarily mean he is not learning it. His other responses will show if he is doing so. It does not matter if he produces only part of a sentence in the new language, so long as he is using the words correctly. Conversational dialogue can be encouraged, in the first instance, by making use of nouns of the second language, as the child did with his own at the one-word sentence stage. The teacher may say: "Please sit on the chaise"—the child says "I want to stand," and the teacher might reply: "When you have finished standing, please sit on the chaise." At the same time, it is better that a child gain practice and confidence with the "I am at l'ecole today" rather than either struggle with the whole sentence and give up trying to put it together, or produce an error and feel stupid.

This method also establishes "correct" items in the child's memory store, rather than incorrect ones, and at the same time helps her to sort out the categories of her new language in relation to her understanding. Differences of sentence structure, as well as the peculiarities, should be discussed *after* the child has a basic command of the language, just as they are discussed in school a few years after she begins to learn his first language. As long as the child understands that "La plume de ma tante" sounds right, but "ma tante's plume" does not, she has no need to try to work out the specifics at this stage. This can come when her understanding of the language and her analytical abilities are both more highly developed; as the Ireland, et al., study (1981) pointed out, it is questionable whether the analytic approach to teaching a second language, even at the gr. 4–6 level, promotes synthesis, as it does not help children to put words together which express their thoughts adequately when they have both the need and the opportunity.

Reading and writing are very much more complex functions than hearing and speech, although both subsume the latter two (Luria, 1966). The child should not be expected to read and write the language until he has acquired some ability to speak it, at least to the stage where he can spontaneously produce simple sentences. His reading and writing should be related to his speaking ability by having him compose his own sentences and then write them down.

One might suggest then that an ideal method of teaching the target language would be to replicate the developmental stages of language acquisition as indicated above, which, given the maturity of the brain, should occur more rapidly the second time. This would then program the cortical association areas in a similar manner to the way in which it acquired its first language, which is the way in which children who learn two languages simultaneously from birth appear to manage it (Kessler, 1971). While some people might argue that it is now "too late" to follow this pattern, on the assumption that the nature of the brain changes at this later age, it can also be argued that the reason that all learning seems to be more effective when one progresses from the simple to the complex is that the brain is "wired up" to assimilate learning in that manner at any age. In a classroom where this method of teaching prevails, there would be no laid-down curriculum or formal programming. The materials and activities provided would be such that the children could develop at their own pace, and within the range of their own activities, to a large extent.

The teacher who has insight into the child's needs and developmental level will be able to determine what is educationally appropriate to each student, and thereby is best able to become the mediator through whom the child develops his cognitive framework. This gives the child an active participation in her own learning, rather than being just a passive receiver of information. Parrotting words and phrases teaches her very little. The mutual questioning, listening, criticizing and all other aspects of teacher-child interaction give the child a greater understanding of the target language, while at the same time giving the teacher a greater understanding of the child's requirements, so the educational framework and goals can be re-formulated where necessary.

It is essential that the teacher make use of the child's first language in helping produce a conversational model for the child's second language, so there is no separation between the first and second languages. There would be no separations for the teacher either, who should teach both languages, so that goals and strategies would be developed in relation to the listening and talking capacities of the children. The interaction resulting from dealing with familiar play materials and objects from the child's natural environment develops an awareness of how these are dealt with in the target language. The child can already converse about these things, so the meaning is already established and can be more easily linked to the new linguistic categories.

Immersion Language Learning for New Immigrants

The second group of children mentioned earlier, new immigrant children learning a second language in order to cope with school and society, present different and more complex problems. In order to deal with these most effectively, new immigrant children should be divided into three subgroups within the school milieu.

- those who are in the 7–9 age range, who have had some schooling in their native lands, have reached the same levels as any other child of that age in linguistic ability, but have learned in a language other than the target language.
- those who are under 7 but have had some formal schooling in their homelands.
- those who are under 7 and who have not previously attended school. In this group, from 4–6 years old, there may also be many who have been born in Canada or the U.S. but who have been exposed only to the language of their parents' ethnic group.

In the first of these sub-groups, there are two problems—that of acquiring the target language necessary for school and that of making sure the child is not unduly retarded in academic progress as a result of his lack of the school's language. These children are also in a state of "culture shock" in many cases, as they suffer all the fears and insecurities concomitant with the massive changes which immigration brings into their lives. The most essential part of their transitional stage is the support of their own language and customs. In the same manner as the Canadian-born child should be able to use his own language while acquiring another, so should these children. They need to be allowed to hear the new language while responding in their own, to work at familiar tasks and manipulate familiar objects while learning how these are dealt with in the target language.

This may appear to be a large order, because it means there must be people who speak the child's language constantly available within this setting. However, the major linguistic groups for immigrants even in Canada, for example, are not so numerous but that the majority, at least, could be provided with interaction with bilinguals fluent in both the child's language and the target one. Such people would not have to be certified or degreed school teachers; intelligent laymen, with a small amount of training, could converse, explain, encourage, interpret and interact with the child, as well as with the teacher, to give him what he needs. Several intensive months of this would give the child a great deal of language, obtained in the optimal manner in terms of his brain-processes, and reinforced by his environmental interactions with other children and situations both in and out of school. If he has already begun to understand the concepts of reading and writing in his first language, he can, when able to make target-language sentences, be encouraged to link these skills to the rest of his linguistic hierarchy.

This experience, given empathetic and perceptive teachers, could help the child to understand more easily Canadian norms and expectancies in a shorter time than is usually the case. The support of her language and culture would result in the child's being aware that there is a respect for what she is, rather than the implicit suggestion that she is "foreign" in some derogatory sense, as is so often the case. This would help her to gain confidence and emotional strength.

At the same time, the bilingual adults, whether acting as teachers or as interpreters for teachers and children, would be able to investigate the child's capabilities properly and instill the necessary learning of curriculum, using the child's first language until he is able to cope with the second. With such interpretation, loss of school progress could be reduced to a minimum. If nothing else, it might reduce some of the "stupid immigrant" notions which so often become the child's own self-image during this traumatic settling-in time. Teaching in the child's first language could continue in key academic areas, tapering off gradually as the children became more fluent in English no matter what their age.

For the second sub-group, children who, although they have been at school for a while in their native countries, are still not 7 years old, a similar program could be arranged; and it may well be that such children, being younger and less influenced by their previous schooling, would progress much more quickly towards efficiency in the target language. They could be given intensive play-manipulation-conversational interaction, without specific curriculum or special concern for academic skill. In other words, they could learn their second language in an intensive manner, by the methods outlined above, but the bilinguals dealing with them would not give prime importance to their academic progress at this stage. When they reach 7 or thereabouts, they could enter the type of classroom outlined above.

Until then, a large group of such children, preferably with various first languages, could be grouped within one such "multi-lingual multi-age grouping kindergarten", given that each linguistic group would have a helper or teacher who is bilingual in both first and target language for that group. This is a little bit easier at this age level, when teacher-child ratios are generally at least a little lower, and as there is not the need to transmit specific academic information which would require the use of "real" teachers. In addition, the advantage of such a multi-age grouping, where the children might range from 5+ to 7+, would be that brothers and sisters might be in the same classroom, which would provide an additional comfort in a new place. It would also encourage the older ones to help the younger ones, not just at school, but in practising at home—talking about what they did in school that day, for example—in their new language as it evolves.

For the sub-group of children from about 4 to 6 who had not yet been to school in their own countries, it is certainly desirable that pre-school training in the language of the school be given. However, one must consider also that the child's stage of development requires a simple and natural approach. Learning will be accomplished best within the play situation, as it would be within the child's natural environment. Again, the teacher does not have to be professionally qualified, nor does the classroom need to be a sophisticated, formally-equipped room. It might, for example, be most easily accomplished from a community centre base, where mothers would be invited to come for a short while each day to learn English themselves while their young children were playing in another room. Taking the children for walks in the neighbourhood and visits to playgrounds, giving them toys and games and helping them interact with these and with each other, using those types of stimuli and situations which they meet in everyday situations and which they are already beginning to understand, is the only sensible way to immerse them in a second language. It must not be forgotten that the reason for their acquiring the school language is sheer necessity and thus it must be made as pleasurable as possible.

The most important factor to remember in planning play programs as a base to second language learning is that these children need a great deal of time to listen to and absorb the target language, to go through the stages of its acquisition, to build up the neurological correlates which enable the brain to operate efficiently in that language. They need to be able to set their own pace and to use the new language by their own choice.

Just as children of any age group show varying degrees of sophistication in their first language, so will these children acquire their second language to varying degrees of efficiency over the time span involved. Attempts to bring them all up to the same level at the same time, perhaps by use of some standardized measurement, will result in anxiety, confusion, and a possible "backlash" effect, where the child fails to learn as he might have. More time must be allowed for these children to develop proficiency;

at the same time, the stage of development of the individual child should never be forgotten. A multi-age grouping makes this far easier, as age need not be the operative factor in moving a child from one classroom to another.

It can be argued that the logistics and financing of such programs make them infeasible; obviously there would be higher costs, since such a method of teaching a second language could at least double the number of adults in primary and junior classrooms. However, a great many of the children now in special programs and/or special education classes might be found to be able to progress very well if they were only given a better grounding in the language which they are struggling to learn. Such grounding would allow their brains to be programmed in a manner which would enable them to sort out the target language from their habituated first language. We suspect that such programs would, if pilot tested, quickly prove their usefulness at reducing long-term special education costs as well as at adapting children quickly, compassionately, and thoroughly to their second language.

In many cases this has not been accomplished in the existing school system, even where it is accepted by all concerned that fluency in the language and competency in assimilating its meaning are prime prerequisites for academic success. The results have been well documented over the past 15 years in the large urban school boards: a large percentage of students from homes in which English is not the first language never quite attain the skills which make academic success in advanced level high school programs possible, and thus are either streamed into general, non-post- secondary-entry courses, or into basic or vocational schools. Too often such students quit school, frustrated and discouraged, and are forced into menial jobs. Such a loss of potential obviously cannot be afforded by our society; immigrant families come not only to "get ahead" in their new land but also to be able to contribute, and lack of total fluency in language skills is a major barrier to such a goal. The initial outlay for such programs would, then, be a small price to pay in terms of its value not only to the children, but to the society as a whole.

There are several other factors which should be considered when programs for teaching second languages to children who come from non-majority languages are being planned. Central among these is that lack of reinforcement for a second language in a family which does not speak it at all is one of the factors which limits vocabulary growth and acquiring competency in usage skills. It also makes it much harder for the child to feel admired and emotionally supported by his parents—the pictures with the words in English carefully printed beneath them for the first time are likely to be intimidating to the mother who doesn't speak English and realizes that soon she and her child may not speak the same language. She knows it is important to learn English, but she probably already realizes that in many cases, learning the new language results in a child who wants to "be Canadian" and who may well stop using his first language as a result. Unless language instruction in the first language is available somewhere in the community, or the school has a heritage language program, such a child may end up not being either fluent or literate in his first language; it gets arrested at the level it was when he entered school. We have even known children who literally could not understand their own parents by the time they reached high school.

Equally difficult is the position of the English-speaking child who comes from another culture, who has strong idiomatic and dialectic habits; often only someone from their own culture who is fluent in "school" English as well can realize the differences between what the child is learning and the habituated, familiar usage of expression to which he has been exposed since birth:

> The importance of taking into account the possible effects of socioaffective centering of input of child verbal performance cannot be overemphasized. When child speech is not entirely consonant with that of the speakers to whom the child is being compared (say, the teacher or certain other children in the community), one may simply assume that the discrepancy is the result of delayed or incorrect learning: it is entirely possible that due to certain sociolinguistic circumstances the child prefers to acquire forms other than those used as the norm. This very important distinction between *cannot* learn versus *prefers not* to learn must be made before it is justifiable to conclude that the child's speech is the result of learning disabilities (Dulay, et al., in Ritchie, 1978, p. 69).

It is, perhaps, unfortunate that these writers have used the term *prefers not*, as if the child is making a conscious choice. This may also be seen as the child being "willful" in a negative sense, resulting in lack of sympathy for his predicament. It must be realized that such a child has had his brain programmed by habituated input of linguistic patterns which make it difficult for him to assimilate "school" English and is not acting from some conscious preference—he is behaving in the only way he can, given his cognitive structure at the time. He must be treated as if, to a large extent, he needs to understand English as it is used in schools as a second language.

There is, however, often suspicion or resistance on the part of the parents of such children, who resent the suggestion that the school thinks they don't speak the "right" English, and presume that English-as-a-second-dialect classes are another form of thinly-veiled racism. Their suspicions may be justified; a fairly recent study by the Toronto Board of Education found that only 36% of black students are enrolled in courses which would allow them to enter university (compared to 54% of the student population overall), slightly more than 28% (Toronto Board of Education, 1988) are attending basic level schools, and disproportionate numbers have ended up in some sort of special education class. In cases insufficient ability to read, write, and speak in "school" English may be a factor in such placement decisions, and "parents feel that when Black children are streamed they lose self-esteem, they lose self-confidence and they continue to choose the less challenging levels in the educational system" (Toronto Board of Education, 1988, p. 26). The parents need to be well informed about schools and programs to offer effective guidance and support to their children.

In fact, one of the major differences in the emotional adjustment of French immersion children versus English as a second language/dialect children is that often middle class Canadian parents do know at least a little French, and their emotional attitude toward immersion schooling, which they have chosen, often at the price of some inconvenience, is very supportive. This attitude is communicated to the child—she is "special," what she is learning is valued and important, perhaps she is trotted out to "perform" for relatives and friends—and obviously this affects her feelings and her progress in the classroom.

This essay will, we hope, serve as a spark for both critical (in the best sense of the word) discussions and, careful research on existing immersion programs, in terms of teaching methods, underpinnings in neurological functioning, cultural and national desirability, effect on achievement in non-language subjects, and optimum timing for the start of such programs. It is not our intention to suggest, in spite of the devil's advocate position taken in some places, that immersion French schooling is not a desirable alternative within the Canadian educational system. Clearly it is always a positive experience to have the deepening and broadening experience of not only learning a second language, but being able to view its culture, so to speak, through it; this is especially true when the two cultures are intrinsically intertwined within one nation.

We would also hope, however, that the desire to promote bilingualism does not result in non-provision or underfunding of English as a second language programming, immersion and otherwise. The two present a somewhat ambivalent contrast: French immersion is seen as academically, culturally, economically and psychologically valuable for children, whereas English immersion of immigrant children is often seen as destructive to self esteem, to native language skills and to family solidarity, and, although culturally and economically essential, is viewed as a grim necessity in many cases. We would like to see planning for such programs include a large dose of compassion and psychological support for young children, as their bilingualism is not only a desirable alternative, but an essential one, if both they and their new country are to thrive.

In the best of all possible worlds, to paraphrase Voltaire's Candide, bilingualism would not be seen as anything less than an enlightening accomplishment for any citizen, of any country, in any time.

Chapter 10

READING: MISERY OR MAGIC?

Reading is a drag. Reading is not as good as television. Reading is something you have to do in order to pass in school. Reading is too hard. Reading makes my head dizzy. Reading is miserable. These are comments many teachers hear daily in their classrooms. Certainly reading, something most of us enjoy or take for granted as adults, has become a major problem in the schools. It is not uncommon to find that one-quarter to one-third of all children entering grade seven are two to three years below standardized norms. The reasons are many and varied; the tendency of parents is to blame whatever method their child was taught to read by, or a poor grade 1 teacher, or immaturity, or too large a class—and all of these may in fact have contributed to a child's or a classes' difficulties. If we are really to approach the problem of reading constructively, however, we must go back further than grade 1—we must look at what underlies the formal process of learning to read, if we are to make it possible for children to learn to read well, and to enjoy doing so.

Reading is a process which begins long before the child comes to school; it begins, in fact, when the child first becomes able to differentiate himself from his mother and begins to play with the idea of being separate from her. As the young child plays peek-a-boo with his mother and recognizes that she has not disappeared forever, he is gradually building up a conceptual framework we call object constancy. This is the image that the child holds in his head when the object disappears. Whereas a child of four or five months may play eagerly with a rattle, if it is removed from his sight, he looks puzzled, perhaps, but then forgets about it. It is as if it no longer exists for him since he can no longer see it. Somewhere near the end of the first or start of the second year, the child becomes able to represent in his head the things he sees and experiences, and to hold on to that image or representation after he no longer sees it. Now, if something is hidden, he will search diligently for it—a missing toy, a dropped cup, or his vanished mother—because he knows it exists even though he cannot for the moment see it.

It is at this developmental level that mental operations really get into full swing for the child; her learning no longer has to be of the trial-and-error method with concrete objects—now she can manipulate images and ideas in her head, she can begin to think about things, rather than react to them. No child will be able to learn in any formal sense until she has fully developed object constancy; she must be able to carry images in her mind and to start using these images in ways which allow her to develop and discover relational qualities among them. She cannot do this when she still has to attend specifically to each concrete object, but only when she is able to remember their abstract images, and the relationships between them.

In the first year and a half or so of life, before much of his verbal language skill exists, then, the child has already developed an awareness of relationships between the familiar objects and people of his environment. It is difficult to know how the infant codes or sorts these, but one has only to watch a baby of 18 months or so, who begins to bounce up and down as an adult approaches the stereo with a record in hand, or to reach as a box of cookies is produced, or to cry as he is carried down the hall toward his bedroom, to realize that the child already knows a great deal about his environment and can predict, or connect, many of the knowings in quite involved ways. The child uses clues to gather meanings about his world, even at this early stage, and constantly explores, physically and verbally, as he begins to learn to put verbal sounds together to signify things to himself and his family. This early exploration of his environment is almost totally through play—play with his own body, anything he can put onto or into himself, and anything he can possibly touch or move. For several years the child spends most of his waking hours playing—and learning.

Before a child is ready formally to learn to read, however, two significant groups of factors must be present, developmentally: both of them stem, basically, from these early play experiences, if adequate stimulation, materials, and freedom to explore are provided by her environment. First, the child must have sufficient sensory-motor development to be able to manage both large and small muscles and to co-ordinate her eye and her hand, and she must be able to focus on objects that she brings close to her and those that are far away. It is of interest to note here that children who come from so-called disadvantaged homes do not show any need for remedial reading if they are given the first two years of school to focus on muscle activity of the torso and limbs, as Miller and Swanson

(1960) have shown. This kind of activity, provided through play, permits the child not only to acquire the above functions and to master them, but also to begin to explore *diagonality* and related visual discrimination, and to have a firm sense of *laterality,* that is, a sense of herself in space. She must know her left hand from her right, and she must have an awareness of grasping and capacity for performing skilled motor functions.

This is essentially a body image picture of herself, and in many children this does not come about until six or seven years of age. It is mirrored by a child's expanding art work, her pictures of what people look like in terms of limbs, dimensions, and relationships between parts. The child must not have continual body-space confusion, otherwise she will not be able to orient her visual focus from left to right and have it remain that way—and we consider this to be one pre-requisite for reading. Motor skill development, sensori-motor competency, visual discrimination and the development of body image all require that the child play in her world. Play is the learning area for the development of reading: a child must play if she is to read with competency, fluency, and understanding. An understanding of her physical world and the physical-spatial dimensions are only acquired by a child through her play with the materials that teachers present to her, materials she finds herself in her play areas, materials her peers provide for her, and most importantly, materials her home has made available for her.

The second group of skills which are of importance before reading can begin are those which make up linguistic competency. The child must be raised in an atmosphere where linguistic symbols are well used and are meaningful in the daily life of the family. In order to experience instructional conversation meaningfully at school, he must come from a verbally oriented home—one where he has had the opportunity to hear concepts verbalized. The environment must be one which encourages him to question, and where his questions are responded to, because he must have the ability to formulate questions in order to gather data about the concepts of his world.

He receives, in this kind of environment, a training in listening to a variety of verbal material, and the opportunity to test out his listening capacities by asking questions and by observing and listening to adult language use—rhythm, phonation, and syntax. The child learns to attend to the sequences of sound, and to anticipate the sequence of language and thought made possible now by his knowledge of the context and syntactical regularities of language in his environment. Knowing this, we can see why children who come to school speaking a language other than English have such difficulty learning to read; *first* it is necessary for them to establish this linguistic foundation all over again in English.

When the child enters the classroom this foundation of visual motor/ spatial/linguistic skills must exist, in the same language as that in which he is going to be asked to read, if he is to learn to do so. If he has these skills, he has a grasp of expressive language, receptive language, and the ability to begin to abstract and generalize about words and questions. In other words, this child has moved from the concreteness of single functional definitions of the things in his environment. Instead of saying that "a block is a piece of wood to play with," the child can talk about a block as a thing which represents wood or brick or stone, and which can be part of a building or a castle or a wall; he can see the multiplicity of uses and can speak of other things as blocks as well—empty shoe boxes, or large pillows, or even sections of a building he sees moved into place by a huge crane.

This abstractness in language usage permits the symbolic approach to problems. Now the child is apt to approach the problem of reading with several sequences. He can see a flow of words, so he does not stop at the end of the first letter, but carries the letter image in his head, and goes from left to right unerringly. He has developed the ability to follow sequences of experienced events and now follows sequences of words. He does not attend to spaces between letters and words. He has found out that printed language matches spoken language in that it has order, rhythm, and sequence—all this he has learned through playing and living in the environment his family has created for him, and now he likes to take books and "play" at reading too. He pretends to read to the doll, without really reading the words, but by making up his own story as he goes along. Thus the visual and auditory discrimination which are rudiments of reading and which precede reading have all been acquired through the process of living his pre-school years.

As the child plays with reading under the guidance of the teacher, she begins the task of discriminating and distinguishing letter forms and associating these with sounds. She uses the letters in play by sorting, classifying and ordering them—all those with tails in one pile, all those without in another—making finer and finer classifications as she masters the primary sequences. It is always with the teacher as catalyst and guiding person that these discoveries are made; she must allow the child to concentrate on the task until she shows a mastery of it, and then introduce finer discrimination tasks along with the sounds for each letter.

It is not until the child grasps the concept that this particular squiggle on the page is a letter, which stands for one or more sounds, and that these letters, when combined, equal words which stand as symbols for the things and people with which she is already familiar, that she is ready to *really* begin reading. Quite some while before this, because we live in a word and symbol-saturated society, she will probably recognize on sight particular words, like her own name, or Coke and McDonald's, with which she is familiar, usually at least partly because of their shape and color and accompanying logos; but the ability to recognize these is not really reading until this concept of the relationship of letters and sounds making up words which have meanings is clearly understood.

As the child is sorting and classifying, he should also be copying shapes, and this kind of play experience improves later reading performance. It is at this time that the teacher can introduce him to a loose-leaf book where he can keep his work and review his progress daily with her. She helps him to have pictures and letter sounds, to make drawings and letter sounds, to write his name when he asks for it, and she is always ready to go back a bit to help reassure the child that it is okay to review his work and not feel he is a failure.

There is no one method that is *the most* successful way to teach reading. Generally research programs agree that children do not learn because of a particular method, but because they evolve strategies for themselves. The teacher and classroom which permit the child to evolve individual strategies will quicken the task and make it seem easier for the child. The strategies he will learn to use will be of the same learning style he has used to master play activities of the sensori-motor and spatial type. He might use trial and error, clues and signs to search for, or clues through the kind of response and sequence he obtains by using them.

Essentially, he searches for rules and meaning to help establish a conceptual framework for written language which he already has internalized, unconsciously, from earliest infancy. It is easy to see, therefore, that the child with visual and auditory competencies which are well developed before he begins to learn to read will read with much more ease than the child who does not have this foundation. A child whose family's language is stunted—repetitive, a limited vocabulary, a good deal of slang and/or community/regional idiomatic usage, non-standard syntax, grammar, or pronunciation, ritualistic and too brief responses to children's questions (in the extreme, this might be "there jest ain't no call for you-all to know that")—is likely to have a far more difficult time developing reading competency.

Reading develops through real experiences and the search for meaning in the world. That is why children must be permitted to use many media and must be given the opportunity to respond to things that interest them, and to express their ideas through drawings, paintings, modelling, movement, scribbling, and drama. When the child is doing, she is learning, and as long as the classroom permits doing she will learn. Bruner (1976) has stated that the child learns by the problems he poses for himself in play better than we could ever teach him any other way. The child, he says, uses his knowledge of language to explain what he is doing, and then gradually he is able to explain without doing the action. This requires much mastery of language and syntax, and is really the abstractness of language, the raw material for reading. His spoken language may be transcribed by the teacher and put into his book; he thus develops the necessary word recognition skills and makes discoveries about the printed words he has used in speech.

We are not entirely sure just how a child learns to read. We know that if the child talks late she will probably have reading troubles, but this only confirms our thoughts about the link between language and reading without telling us about reading per se. The child will probably make many errors in her first attempts to print. These errors indicate that she is trying to interpret print, and provide several clues as to how the child operates as well. One child, for example, may concentrate on the shape of a letter or word, while another always gets the beginnings or endings right even when the middle is inaccurately transcribed. This would seem to show that children use different clues for learning words: some use shapes, some similarities in form, and other individual letters as the key to remembering what the word is and how to write it.

What is important is that each child must be given the time and opportunity to explore, to discover, and to develop her own methods for discriminating letters and words—no one method will work equally well for every child. Each child's explorations will be uniquely her own, because the words and the ideas she uses have come from the real experiences she has had. The teacher can help best, not by prescribing one method, but by writing letters and words, on request, and assisting in the process of discrimination and comparison as the child formulates her own method.

Children quickly learn to enjoy playing with the printed word as they enjoyed playing, earlier, with objects and with the spoken word—the fun of patterning and grouping and re-arranging and repeating—manipulating words as they did blocks only a few short years before. They rhyme words, add pieces at the beginning and end, make their own anagrams and crossword puzzles, make up new words with private meanings which they can change at will. They collect, sort, order and classify in many different piles, by color, or length, or alphabetical order, or endings—by meanings, by season, by activity, or by sound. As they master these activities, they ask for more. The teacher must then anticipate children's academic needs and broaden the classroom to act not only as a stimulator but also as a means for them to get satisfaction of their growing curiosity in this very important area. Maps, pictures, books of every description and of varied difficulty and a wide range of interest, not only those traditionally thought of as suitably academic, can spur children on to further growth as people by opening out their world.

We can provide an adequate grounding of visual/motor/spatial/ linguistic competency to each child by allowing children to explore and manipulate their young world through play, both at home and in pre-school and primary classrooms. We can build a foundation carefully, with sensitive teachers who allow children to approach reading in their own way and without pressure to "be like the others," to hurry or to perform. If we can accomplish these two things, then we *can* replace that not uncommon reaction to reading as a feared drudgery, a misery, with the excitement of reading as a magic carpet to anywhere, and always, for all our children.

PART FOUR
USING PLAY AS A
DIAGNOSTIC AND THERAPEUTIC TOOL

For many children being a "kid" is not the special time we as adults typically remember it to be. Many children, for example, suffer from the symptoms of childhood depression. As well, there are those children, who for a variety of reasons, are not developing normally either clinically or cognitively; a large number of these come from homes whose family dynamics impeded normal development. There are children who have been removed from their families and sent to institutions outside of their community. Is there any way we can help these children as they appear in day care, nursery, school, and camp settings?

The chapters that make up Part Four (Chapters 11 to 13) of this book are concerned with the use of play as an effective diagnostic and therapeutic tool. Chapter 11 outlines some of the predisposing factors related to clinical depression in childhood. The chapter also addresses the childhood depression that results from the loss of a parent. Chapter 12 provides some direction for teachers and other working with children who are not developing normally either emotionally or cognitively. Chapter 13 discusses the rationale against the institutionalization of children. This chapter also provides an overview of possible therapeutic alternatives to institutionalization.

Chapter 11

LOSS, ANGER, GRIEF, GUILT: THE CYCLE OF DEPRESSION IN CHILDHOOD

"I feel so low today!"
"I've got the blues again."
"I just couldn't get out of bed, the world seemed so bleak."
"When I lost that job, my world just fell apart."
"After my marriage broke up, I was a zombie for months."
"There just doesn't seem to be any point to life."
"The year that my mother died seemed endless, just months of tears."
"It's like a gray fog which hangs over my head."
"I feel so alone, even when there are people around me."

Sound familiar? Probably everyone has had days when they've said, or heard, lines like these, because depression touches everyone, at least briefly, at some point during their lives. For some it is just a bad day, or a reaction to a life event which didn't work out the way one had hoped, or the result of overwork, stress, lack of vacation time. Many people feel it in the loss or absence of a close and supportive relationship. Sometimes it may be part of the aftermath of a serious physical illness or surgery. For some it might be a reaction to the long months of winter, of grayness and being closed in: the modern equivalent to the "cabin fever" of the early pioneers. Sometimes it is the result of too many changes in too short a time period—a job change, a child leaving for university, a transfer to a new city. For most it accompanies the death of someone they have been close to, particularly family members.

Such depression is, in fact, a very normal reaction to loss or perceived loss of something important. And for most people, its duration is limited; the grief is profound, the loss is mourned, the change is adapted to, and finally one morning the sky does seem blue again and life goes on. Morrissey, Klerman and Goldman (1980) observed that depression manifested in such a fashion, as a mood in response to external catalysts, represents an aspect of normal human experience.

Grief can perhaps best be defined as an inwardly-directed reaction to loss in which tears, sadness, apathy, lack of appetite, inability to sleep, or,

143

conversely, feeling the need to sleep all the time, and lack of energy or will to keep going may all play a part.

Clinical depression, the psychopathology which we call a depressive state, however, is not so simply a response, and not at all simply resolved. Felix Brown (1966) defined it thus: "when a patient is unhappy and becomes ill in some way *through* this unhappiness, he can be said to be suffering from a depressive state." Such a state often seems out of balance with the precipitating loss, or lasts far longer than one might consider "normal"; the person suffering in a depressive state seems to have little or no ability to shake it off or to respond flexibly to other stimuli within his environment. It seems almost predetermined and selfperpetuating, as an enduring mood which transfers across all the functions of a person's life. Unresolved, it may well last months, or, in some cases, be an underlying factor in the person's approach to the world for years.

Although of all psychological terms, "depression" has most clearly entered the language as a term with a generally understood meaning, it may be useful to further define it. Paul Trad (1987) does so quite usefully when he distinguishes between depression as an *affective state*, "the external representation of the subjective experience of emotion . . . which may be a symptom of a depressive disorder or of a host of other disorders"; depression as a *mood*, "the predominant conscious, subjective emotion which colors one's perception of the world"; and depression as a *syndrome*, a "cluster of symptoms causing varying degrees of incapacity, having a commonly occurring clinical picture, a natural history, a number of biochemical correlates, and a predictable response to treatment" (p. 26).

Those who work with children as child care workers, early childhood workers, teachers, and social workers, frequently report that children in their care are "depressed"; often this is a common sense observation based largely on the child's behaviour: facial expressions, verbalizations, body language, lack of energy, irritability, sleep problems, bed wetting, and so forth. Their assumption is that many of the same behaviours which they recognize as depression in adults must also be true of depression in children. And often the cause of the depression is obviously situational and recent, and, as in adults, the depression gradually ends. But sometimes it doesn't, and sometimes the cause is not so obvious; for professionals dealing with such children, this is both saddening and frustrating, as too often they feel hopeless and helpless in the face of the child's profound sadness. The underlying assumption of this chapter is that understanding the causes of such depression may aid those who deal with such children in devising strategies to help them learn to cope with and overcome it.

The currently accepted professional approach to diagnosing depression in childhood is based on the adult criteria in *Diagnostic and Statistical Manual of Mental Disorders, Third Edition* (American Psychiatric Association, 1980). The symptomology listed for major depressive episodes for children includes a dysphoric mood, characterized by a depressed or sad affect, hopelessness, and/or irritability, plus at least three of the following four symptoms in children under six years: failure to make expected weight gain, insomnia or hypersomnia, hyperactivity, and signs of apathy.

The weakness of this listing, according to Trad (1987), is that it offers no suggestion of the origins of infant and childhood depression, or of the role that temperamental factors or the attachment relationship may contribute to fostering depression, and focuses instead on depression at a point where it is a full-fledged syndrome, rather than on depressive-like phenomena which may predict later depressive bouts. He maintains that a more developmental model should be used, as this adult-like approach too often is not useful in diagnosing or treating childhood depression, particularly in that it does not account for nonverbal ratings, or for discrepancies between sources, such as parent and child. Thus Trad's developmental model includes a number of predisposing factors for depression in the life of an infant or young child.

This chapter will reflect to some degree the causative factors Trad outlines, but also on their impact beyond early childhood, and on depression as a reaction to an experience of loss in childhood.

The early studies done by John Bowlby (1969) developed the theory that the loss of a beloved person by death leads to faulty personality development and emotional illness which, of course, includes depression as an illness and as a forerunner to graver ills. He stated: "First, in the childhoods of depressives, loss is likely to be due to the death of a parent. Second, although in depressives the bereavement tends to be raised during each five years of childhood, losses tend to occur frequently in patients aged 10–15. Third, the incidence of loss is apt to be most raised for the parent of the opposite sex." He points out that loss of a parent by death between the 10th and 15th birthdays tends to occur twice as frequently in a group of depressives as it does in the population as a whole.

What happens when such a loss takes place? There has been a wide range of disagreement among leading authorities on the question of a child's capacity to grieve. Anna Freud (1953) suggested that mourning could not occur before the age of six years; in contrast, Bowlby (1960) hypothesized that even as early as six months a child can grieve. Trad (1987) concludes that "although full fledged depressive symptomatology may not be manifested for prolonged periods of time prior to six months of age, the developmental process, whereby the infant integrates patterns of response, may become part of the regulatory process well before 6 months of age" (p. 24).

Notwithstanding the lack of agreement among these and other authorities as to when a child first grieves, it is clear that it does occur even in very small children. If we can accept the notion that babies are capable of sensing loss of a loved person, we can learn something from the grief of older children who may, or may not, become depressives in later years. We need to examine the process of reality testing which underlies normal development in order to understand grief in childhood.

When a child is very small, he or she experiences the anxiety of being separated from parents at bed time and when they go out for a few hours. Gradually she comes to trust them—and life—and she realizes that her parents will be there upon her waking and that they will return from their outings. He begins to learn that just thinking strange and probably terrifying thoughts will not cause them to happen: he is not a slave to his fantasies. All this is the emergence of a capacity to expect and to predict, to hope and to expand thinking, and the child begins to build his or her self image upon these emotional fundamentals, in which are incorporated the people and events which influence his world.

The growing child gradually becomes more capable of handling the complexities of the world outside: "Much as we love you, you may not have three candy bars a day—you cannot go to the movies six times a week—if you only have 64 cents left of your allowance, you cannot buy four new Transformers." And this pragmatic reality, the invisible give and take of everyday life, is forever being nibbled at by children, for they are always testing us and life. To the extent that we stick rigidly to the rules, relax them too far, or effect a loving compromise, children will grasp reality more or less adequately, together with the surety of parental understanding.

As the child becomes better able independently to carry out her own reality testing without reference to her parents, the beloved objects, the parents, who led her into this more mature stage, become permanently incorporated into her maturing self-picture. Thus a very great deal of emotional energy, of libido, is tied up in these beloved objects, and it can be said that the child, incorporating this object with herself, has invested a very high proportion of her emotional capital in this relationship. So when a child loses someone by death, the loss will be fiercely felt, and the child will grieve most deeply.

After the initial shock of a parent's death, how will the young child react? As Freud pointed out more than seventy years ago, "reality testing has shown that the loved object no longer exists, and it proceeds to demand that all libido shall be withdrawn from its attachment to that object" in Strachey, (1967). This withdrawal can only be achieved in a fragmented way, for it is a most agonizing process: as most of us know, in times of loss, no one grieves constantly and deeply without relief—rather, we go through a number of fluctuating phases with recurring peaks of sorrow.

Gradually the libidinal feelings of the child toward the lost person are withdrawn, and, as this takes place, the child will begin to feel anger towards the lost, loved person. For he has relied on and trusted that person in a very special way and has invested a very great deal of himself, so that person who died, has, so to speak, let him down. So the bereaved child is truly angry about the death, angry with the person for dying. But this anger is almost always short lived, and is replaced by guilt—though the child may not be aware of either emotion. Anger changes to guilt because the child, in beginning to acquire mastery over immediate drives and desires, has developed a conscience, a super-ego, and this warns him that anger is dangerous and can destroy people, perhaps someone else in the family which means so much to him.

At this stage we begin to see the vicious circle of the normal child's normal reaction to loss, and we perceive the start of what could lead to a more permanent depressive state. Through guilt, she forces her angry feelings into her subconscious; but these feelings still affect motivation, and the child now has to use energy to quell these angry, aggressive feelings and drives. Thus this energy is unavailable for normal reactions, for it is bound up in maintaining repression. Loss of energy results in withdrawal, and withdrawing prevents normal satisfactions. Depression occurs because of the loss of these satisfactions, anger because of that loss, and, once more, guilt because of the new anger. And so once more depression, anger, guilt, and eventually significant depression with no release, except by release of feeling.

While this process diminishes the child from within, the environment with which he is familiar and comfortable is also changing. Marris, writing in 1958 on widows and their families, pointed out that the remaining parent has the logistical problems of caring for the family in quite a different way; if this is the mother, she may have to work full time and thus the child experiences another loss, albeit not of such a permanent nature. The change in the sense of security and love previously enjoyed by the child or children can lead to an unreal idealization of the lost parent or of the earlier environment. And this puts added strain upon thé only recently developed reality-testing abilities of the child.

As is probably obvious, the loss of a parent through divorce or abandonment precipitates reactions in young children which may be quite similar to those experienced after the death of a parent. The child comes to recognize that the absent parent no longer exists in the same manner as he or she did before: he doesn't live there anymore, isn't part of the routines of the child's life, perhaps even is no longer in the same city or country. The anger the child feels is directed not just at the parent whose absence is mourned, but also frequently at the custodial parent. Particularly if the separation follows hostility and aggression between the parents, the child may blame the present parent for the absence of the other.

And, sadly, too often the child feels guilt not just for her anger, but also feels that she caused the family breakup: perhaps the parents fought about her, about her behavior, about the financial demands of a family, or the constraints it places on parental freedom. The futile hope of the child that somehow she can bring the parents back together and "make it all better" masks the desperation of a child trying not to feel such destructive guilt.

And for many children of such dissolved relationships, the pain continues; whereas the child whose parent is dead gradually loses the "picture" of the lost parent, and often the anger and grief at the loss slowly subside over the years, the children of divorce grapple with reoccurring grief, anger and guilt. Each time the missing parent is seen, or stayed with, parting occurs again, and a resurgence of the pain. Each holiday represents a choice made by the child, or the parent, which while pleasing one parent, pains the other—and the child most of all. Parents who remain hostile hold their children hostage to their anger as they ask young children to choose, to have a favourite, to love one more than the other, to adopt the parent's anger toward the other as the child's own reaction. It is hard to believe that such warring parents cannot see the damage done to the children they both profess to love—but every classroom teacher sees the sad face of the child tossed between two equally loved adults.

Eventually the anger the child feels at both may become too great to be dealt with—the risk is too enormous. If one parent is already gone, can the child risk being openly angry with the other? And the load of guilt is built in the child whose parent keeps reminding him of all the parent has given up, of all the work done, and things gone without for the sake of the child, and of the child's ingratitude at preferring, even silently, the other parent. If one or the other parent remarries, either an individual or another single parent with children, the jealousy and anger, and the resultant guilt at feeling angry when one's parent seems so happy, finally, may be too much for a child to bear.

Often the discrepancy between the lifestyle of the father, who statistically is more likely to be financially well off, and that of the mother, who is very often shoved into poverty by family breakdown, breeds resentment and anger in the child as well. And in angry outbursts, the child may idealize the absent parent; often the more absent, the more idealized: "Daddy wouldn't make me do that; daddy would let me go!" Even children of divorced parents who remain civil or friendly, or who share custody, often feel sad for years, mourning the loss of the happy family which they have idealized in their heads. Some older adolescents eventually come to feel that they, in fact, have no father—just an amiable relative who breezes through town or calls occasionally, good for a little extra money or an extravagant gift, to be coddled somehow: "dad's in town, so I have to at least have lunch with him.—it's ok, I'll go bowling with him, I don't know what else we can do together."

So the child who experiences loss of a parent by divorce may well move through the same process of grief, repressed anger, guilt, and depression as does the child whose parent dies. Depending on the particular circumstances of the family, the child's depression may be resolved over time, or may lead to a more prolonged depressive state.

Hospitalization, especially of young children, is also seen as a major risk factor for depression in childhood; the degree of risk is a function of many factors, such as age at time of hospitalization, length of stay, and type of procedures performed (Nahme-Huage et al., 1977). Infants and children hospitalized early, repeatedly, and for long period of time, face the most serious risk of depression. Simply put, a young child who is hospitalized suffers from a feeling of loss of control as a consequence of a body which doesn't work properly; a sense that his parents are not, as he had thought, omnipotent and all-knowing and able to protect him from harm; the separation from his parents, particularly his mother; and an alien and often seemingly uncaring environment. Anna Freud (1953) wrote that an early life experience is significant to a child not so much because of its external reality as its psychic reality—the realm in which a child's unconscious fantasies operate to give even harmless events a sinister meaning. For many children the experience of illness or hospitalization confirms their most terrifying fears by activating such fantasies.

At the very beginning of the century, high infant mortality rates in institutions such as hospitals and orphanages, while caused partially by lack of medical care, were probably also evidence of the harmful effects of hospitalizing children. Spitz's work (1945) on the effects of long term hospitalization of British infants during World War II explored the problem of devastating psychological damage. Virtually every research study on the adverse effects of sickness and hospitalization includes depressive symtomatology. Clearly, the interaction of three factors triggers such depression and determines its impact on the child over time: the nature of the illness, hospital procedures and practices, and the child's family and social environment.

We should like to focus on the part of the hospitalization process which parallels a child's experience with parental loss by death or divorce; a very young child who is hospitalized has no way of knowing that her parents will return once they leave her hospital bed. She is surrounded by strangers, most of them wearing masks and wielding unfamiliar equipment. She is not in the safety of her own bedroom, with her familiar toys and perhaps her siblings. She is in pain, either severely or intermittently, and many of the things which are meant to make that pain go away only seem to inflict greater pain; she doesn't understand, often, what is wrong with her or what must be done to fix it, or even if it is fixable. Her memories of the broken toy which was thrown away may lead her to feel that since she is broken, she too will be thrown away. Parents reappear, and disappear, and for the very young child this seems totally unpredictable. Too often hospital rules prevent parents from helping to nurse the sick child, or the equipment necessary is too complicated, and siblings are not allowed to visit. The parents are afraid, and the child picks up that feeling, and is terribly frightened; if her parents, whom so far she has experienced as all-knowing, all-powerful, are afraid, what protection does she have left?

The child often comes to feel abandoned, deserted by his mother and father, and is by turns angry at them and misses them. If they do not come when he expects them, he may panic and feel that his anger has driven them away, or destroyed them permanently. Anger doesn't feel right—he knows he should be glad to see them, and they tell him he must do as the doctors and nurses say, and be grateful for their joint care of him—and so the guilt arises. In extreme cases, a terminally ill child who is old enough—perhaps five or six—to do so may feel the need to protect his or her parents from the reality of impending death by denying it, thus losing the chance to be angry at fate and to grieve at the separation to come, both of which are necessary before death can be accepted (Weininger, 1975).

As with loss of a parent by death or divorce, what is activated in the child by such an experience of loss of control, of safety, and of parenting is anger which is dealt with by being repressed—which in turn takes so much emotional energy that the child suffers from depression, from loss of the ability to allow himself to feel and to grieve.

Akin to this is the experience of many, if not most, handicapped children. A handicapped child may, due to the organic nature of the handicap, have difficulty in expressing or acting out the normal feelings and behaviours of a normal infant or child. This inability may condition the response of the parents to the child; unable to see or feel a positive response in their infant to their caring, they may in turn become less able to demonstrate affection or a natural approach to the child as a "real person." In addition, parents of such infants often feel disappointment, inadequacy, frustration, anger, and guilt, which are mixed into their attachment behaviours toward their child; attachment behaviours are those which make for social bonding of mother to child, such as smiling, singing, holding, playing, talking, touching, kissing, and rocking. Their love for the child is mixed with helplessness and depression, as well as, often, the physical fatigue from the amount of care many handicapped infants require; all of these may result in a marked ambivalence for the child. Thus by the time the child achieves a full-fledged sense of self, he or she may already feel stigmatized, a person too different from others to be really lovable or truly human.

Society's response to the visibly profoundly handicapped child is often likely to be avoidance, or an assumption that because the child is in a wheelchair, or looks strange, or can't talk clearly, he or she should be ignored, or spoken to slowly or loudly or treated as an object. The disabled child's need for help in accomplishing bodily functions often leads to the caregiver developing an impersonal approach, especially in institutions, and also leads to the child's embarrassment, especially as he or she nears adolescence, with the need to have others do "babyish" things to or for one. Under these circumstances it is not surprising that such children have difficulty achieving a positive body image or self image (Weininger, Rotenberg & Henry, 1972).

Given the longer hospital stay at birth which results in separation from their mothers, the greater physical and emotional difficulties of caring for handicapped children, and their more frequent, and often longer term hospitalization or institutionalization as they grow up, it is not surprising that many handicapped groups are seen as "at risk" for depression.

One of the problems in assessing the incidence of depression in handicapped children has been the assumptions made about the temperaments of children with particular kinds of handicapping conditions. For example, the quite rigid stereotype that deaf children will almost inevitably be impulsive, hyperactive, rigid, and suspicious, and the assumption that such behaviours are the initial impediment to effective mother-child interactions. Trad (1987) questions whether this is in fact the case, and suggests that behaviours are derived from the early interaction of mother and child, not from the handicapping condition itself.

A review of the research of the last 60 years on the mentally retarded (Sovner & Hurley, 1983) disputes the theory that the retarded lack the psychological capacity to suffer affective disorders. Rather the stereotype of retardation may lead to a blurring of the ability of observers to distinguish between the symptoms of such disorders. In addition, there are real difficulties in studying such children because many may be being treated with drugs which obscure symptomology, and many are already institutionalized, making it difficult to know if depressive disorders stem from the handicap itself or from the nearly total emotional and physical separation from family inherent in such long term hospitalization.

In a somewhat controversial study, Colbert, Newman, Ney and Young (1982) have postulated that many so-called learning disabilities are really manifestations of an underlying depression which decreases a child's capacity for energy and attentiveness, leading to poor school performance. In their study over half the population of children under 15 admitted to a family unit of a hospital—two thirds of whom were above average in intelligence but underachieving in school—were diagnosed as depressed. Underachievement, when diagnosed as resulting from a learning disability, often leads to segregation in special classes, or a move to a non-neighborhood school, which may worsen a child's self image, loosen bonds with neighborhood playmates, lead to stigmatization among age peers, and thus cause increased depression.

The handicapped child can be seen as suffering from a loss of normalcy relations: in the ordinary interactions with parents and other family members in infancy; in normal childhood play activities and peer relationships; in the ability to be "just one of the kids" in a family, a neighborhood or a school; in physical self-sufficiency; in the usual emotional ties of adolescence; in the experience of individual success. The child's growing recognition that he or she will never be "just like everyone else" may well be a source of grief—for the loss of the person one might have been, should have been, wishes to be—and also of anger, a lashing out of "why me?" and finally, of depression, which may be all the more profound because of the child's knowledge that this condition, and the physical or psychic pain and frustration accompanying it, will not ever go away.

Trad (1987) delineates another kind of loss which may precipitate depression in children. He speaks of loss of social support—from the community, the social network (relatives, work associates, friends), and confiding partners or families—as a byproduct of the sweeping changes in the economy and structure of society, as well as the structure of family and community life over the last decades.

Many studies have been done which identify social support as a critical factor in health maintenance; Cohen and Willis (1985) are just two of many who report that both physical and psychological health are affected by the presence or absence of social support networks. The parent who is living in a high-stress environment is at risk, and the child even more so, as he suffers not only the poverty or lack of connectiveness but from the lack of ability of the stressed family to adequately nurture him.

Children from homes experiencing economic and social stress often suffer from a lack of both quantity and quality of stimulation for cognitive growth and emotional nurturance; it is not income per se which causes the problems, rather the stresses and lack of social support for such families which produce the modification of parent behavior. These are clearly evident in single families which are mother-led (MacKinnon, 1982), but they are also present in families where mothers shoulder the triple burden of an outside job, parenting, and housework; such role pressure has been seen to be directly related to depression in employed mothers (Parry, 1982). Parmalee, Beckwith, Cohen and Sigman (1983) found that when economic factors associated with low socioeconomic status contributed to an infant being a low priority in the family, neither medical intervention nor social support were very effective in mitigating depressive symptoms in both mothers and children. Not only does poverty seem to make depression within families more likely, it also makes it substantially more chronic, with longer periods of depression and older age at relapse likely (Kéller, Lanori, Rice, Coryell & Hirschfeld, 1986).

There has always been poverty, of course, although the industrialized societies are comparatively fortunate in this respect; a generally un-recognized factor may be that what causes the stress or pain for many poor families is not only the deprivation, overcrowded housing, lack of food and clothing, but the loss of hope. The great contemporary capital-ist myth is that anyone can succeed, anyone can be wealthy—and those who cannot do so are seen too often not as victims of society but as victims of their own character flaws and economic poor judgement. They are seen as "not trying hard enough—lazy and irresponsible."

The children of the poor absorb this value judgement in school and in the neighborhood and from social service agencies, all of whom should know better; and at the same time, in the media, in the store windows, on the signboards, they see wealth and consumer goodies they know some-how they will never have. Their parents are shamed by the need to ask for help, for food, for subsidies in housing and for such seemingly unimportant things as school trips and recreation for their children. Again, both anger—too often at themselves rather than at the society around them—and guilt—at their own lack of success, lack of ability to control their own lives—result in the repression of all feeling which is depression. And the children feel anger at their parents, who are "supposed" to be able to do better, and guilt at that anger; they come to school, where the structure of the system virtually ensures failure for the children of poverty, and feel guilt at their failure, and anger at the school, the teacher, and most sadly, at themselves, and thus finally depression.

Along with poverty, other major social problems such as alcoholism and drug abuse frequently cause not only economic hardships, but impaired parent and child interactional patterns which result in increased incidence of depression within a family. Parents who are addicted often do not have the ability to focus on their children's needs; the need for the addictive substance often becomes so overwhelming that profound neglect of the children results. Cases where children are sent out to forage for drugs, or deal in them, or even to prostitute themselves to earn money for the parent's addiction are, sadly, not unknown, especially in large urban slum areas where addiction may have become a way of life for a population which has no hope for their future, and no dreams to offer their children.

For many children, whether in slum areas or in "nice" middle class families, parental alcoholism or drug abuse is experienced as deep shame combined with fierce need to "keep the secret"; such children can be seen as mourning a loss of something they may never have had—a normal family, like the ones they see on television, where parents are responsive, protective, predictable, and affectionate. As with other losses, this loss may lead to feelings of anger at parents who do not seem to value them, nurture them, and protect them; of grief at not being able to change their parents, or to alter the realities of their own existence; and eventually, to feelings of depression.

Clearly it should also come as no surprise that children who are abused are very strongly at risk in terms of depression; nearly one-quarter of American families are at risk for abuse: this translates into roughly 40 million American children (Garbarino, 1977), and one can only assume similar trends in other industrialized nations. First of all, the abusing parent warps the interaction between himself/herself and the young child, generating a relationship which is either avoidant or resistant, and lacking in the trust and sense of protection which the developing child must have. Sometimes the older child can "see" what he perceives as the cause of the parent's violence—the alcohol, the lost job, the lack of money, the anger between the parents. But too often the only explanation which fits—often helped along by the parent's need to blame someone else ("If you don't stop making me angry, you'll get what you're asking for!"—"I'm doing this for your own good because you're bad!")—is the child's own lack of worth. If he were truly a good child, a child worth loving, certainly his father wouldn't hit him all the time. For some children even the resulting pain seems preferable to the indifference which they experience the rest of the time; sadly, we have seen children run away from safe and loving foster homes to their own abusing families in search of the "proof" they are used to that they are cared about.

The sexually abusing parent is loved, at least at the beginning, and says, by word or deed, that the sexual behavior is appropriate; the child senses often that it is not, but in the absence of any other model for parental behavior, and as a much smaller person, must accept it. Or perhaps it is the only physically affectionate behavior the child has known. The abusing parent often threatens the child with violence or with blame if the secret is told: "They'll send me away and you'll all have no money and no place to live"—"See what happened to the doll? That's what would happen to you if you told!" The abused child often internalizes the abuse as her own fault, caused by something she did or failed to do, or by her own lack of worth, all of which result in a severe loss of self esteem. She may also feel justifiable anger at both the parent who abused her and the one who did not stop it from happening, did not protect her, did not love her enough to guess that something was wrong. Her guilt may come from feeling angry at her parents, or from the sense that she should somehow have been able to prevent it, or that she enjoyed some of what happened, or from the feeling that she destroyed, if she shared the secret, her idealized happy family. The anger and guilt often lead to long-term impairment of capacity for positive sexual relationships as well as to depression.

A syndrome known as "learned helplessness" also arises here; the child is confused about whether the abuse is his or her own fault, or simply another facet of a world which generally seems incomprehensible and beyond control. Thus gradually he or she develops both a negative sense of self esteem and an impaired sense of causality; actions in the surrounding world, both positive and negative, are seen as a result of luck, chance, or external forces beyond individual control. This engenders a helplessness or apathy, a loss of belief in one's own ability to mitigate the circumstances and events of life. Such an attitude tends to immobilize the child—why try, at school or with friends or at home, when so clearly events beyond one's ability to understand or to alter are to blame?

Clearly, within the framework of world affairs, many adults have fallen victim to learned helplessness—"What can I do about world peace . . . famine . . . disease . . . poverty . . . the government? I'm only one person and I can't change the system" seems somehow to give many adults the permission they need to sit back and attempt nothing, apathetically staring at the disasters they see on the TV. Anger, and any action which one might feel compelled to take as a result of it, is a luxury when such a conditioning world view has been internalized.

It should come as no surprise then that those who are abused—both women and children—so frequently seem to accept this abuse as an unavoidable reality. Frequently the physical damage is secondary to the psychological effects of domestic violence. The child's temperament, sense of object relations, empathic development, and capacity for self-representation are indelibly marred by abuse and neglect. According to some studies, aside from loss or separation of a parent, these are the primary causes of childhood depression (Blumberg, 1981; Garbarino, 1977; Wolfe, 1985).

The earlier discussion of social and economic change and lack of viable social support suggests, of course, factors which impinge on the development of stress and which in turn contribute to the rising incidence of domestic violence, as do alcoholism, drug abuse, and parental psychopathology. One of the most profound results of physical or sexual abuse in a family is an inability on the part of all its members to connect meaningfully to each other—the abused child withdraws rather than seeks out the parent or caregiver, the family is isolated and non-communicative, and the child therefore is less able to respond to warmth or to trust others in the future. Not only this, but as DeLozier (1982) has pointed out, the lack of a secure base of self esteem handicaps a child's development of mastery, which in turn contributes to a sense of depression.

And sadly, the response of children who have been treated violently or without regard to their feelings and needs is too often to become violent themselves; the literature reports clearly elevated levels of aggression and violence among abused children as they grow older and in turn when they are parents. Seemingly the anger such children feel toward the abusing parent, and toward themselves for either causing the anger or being unable to avoid it, and their guilt at being unworthy of their parents' love and protection, may surface not only as depression but ultimately as a continuation of the patterns of abuse and neglect which they themselves suffered.

Another consequence is that this violence is not directed outward, but culminates in childhood or adolescent suicide. Many studies have linked abuse and neglect with children's suicidal behaviour. The combination of isolation and aggression which are common among both abusive and suicidal families suggests that a depressive mechanism may link the two; for example Ackerly (1967) found that family fighting was common to all of the suicidal children he studied, and Winokur, et al (1971) found that alcoholism was a significant factor in both abusive and suicidal family patterns.

Another kind of separation loss which seems to us to precipitate childhood and adolescent depression is that which we would term "transplant shock"; we see this as related in some ways to the loss of social support, but more culture-specifically. Large numbers of immigrant children in middle and late childhood are entering school systems as soon as they enter their new country. Many of them suffer not only the culture shock which anyone exposed to a radically different country feels, in terms of race, religion, political and social structures, language, and technology; rather they are like plants which have been transplanted without sufficient preparation or fertilization, and, lacking such supports, they do not thrive.

Social workers in immigrant agencies and teachers in multicultural schools often report what seems to be a high incidence of depression in such children; often it is not immediate—at first the trauma of the change prevents using energy for anything but rapid adaptation—but rather two or more years later. Typically, the child most affected is one who was uprooted with little or no prior warning and moved, without his extended family, into a radically different culture and climate, with a language very different from English (like Vietnamese, Russian, or Hebrew); this is exacerbated if he looks different or practices a different religion, or if he feels somehow that by leaving his own country he has abandoned it, made it somehow less worthy, and if he cannot go home again for strong political or economic reasons.

At first, and often within two or three years, such a child seems to have adjusted—he can speak English idiomatically, his written work is becoming more articulate, he has caught up in other academic areas, wears all the "right" adolescent clothes, adopts the fast food, movies, TV, and musical habits of the peer group, and has an appropriately North American goal framework. Sometimes the first onset of depressive symptoms is if the child goes back to his original country for a visit; somehow he returns feeling neither what he was nor what he sees he must become—in a kind of "nationality limbo." Or perhaps a relative or old neighbor arrives to visit or stay, and the child realizes how wide the gap has become between the new and the old world for him, and that he can't, and perhaps no longer really wants to, go home again—even if it were politically feasible.

Of course much of this is not new; the adaptation of immigrants to North America has produced a wide variety of studies in the past century detailing the stresses which accompany building a new identity in a new culture. Perhaps the crucial difference is that many of these adolescents lack the propulsion or motivation which once fueled new immigrants; they are not coming, starry-eyed, to a new country where the streets are paved with gold and they will become rich and famous, envied by those they left behind. Rather most of them are political, economic, or religious refugees who left their homes as the only alternative to severe discrimination, imprisonment, torture, or possibly death. And they are very angry at the powers which forced them to leave their homes, their parents who couldn't make them safe, a world which they don't understand, and the new country which too often doesn't want them, denies the dangers they faced, and barely tolerates their presence.

And perhaps they are also experiencing the guilt of the survivor. This was first seen in those who poured out of the refugee camps and concentration camps of World War II Europe—a guilt at their good fortune in escaping the death of their families, friends, countrymen. Many of these children come from eastern Europe, from the refugee camps of southeastern Asia, from South Africa, from the war zones of Latin America and the Middle East; they come very often without much hope, with much guilt at their own survival and comparative safety, and with anger not only for what they have lost but for what cannot be—their hopes for a future in their own countries. It is not surprising, then, that such guilt and anger at themselves, their parents, and at the new country may lead also to depression.

Central to all of the research which has been cited so briefly here is one strand—the strong relationship between a sense of loss in a child's life and resulting depression. The most severe loss, that of a parent or other close family member by death; the related loss of a parent and a family structure through divorce; the loss of control and safety in a hospitalized child; the loss of normalcy for the handicapped child; the loss of security, hope, and social supports in a poor child's life; the loss of parental relationship in an abused child; the loss of roots and faith in an abruptly transplanted child; all of these can be seen as being related to a child's inability to build and maintain relationships which are satisfying and developmentally essential. Such losses contribute to a child's anger and subsequent guilt, and the repression of these feelings leads in turn to depression which immobilizes the child and limits further positive development.

The emotional capital of young twentieth century children is invested within a very narrow compass, their nuclear families, with little chance of diversification; any loss of ability to be emotionally a positive part of the family is, therefore, very damaging and increases the risk for childhood depression. Any loss which prevents the development of a healthy self esteem, and subsequently, strong peer relationships, a place in the community and in society, may also precipitate a depressive state which may well last beyond childhood or adolescence into adulthood. Clearly there are many children at risk, and many causative factors which are beyond the capacity of individual parents, teachers or therapists to change. But an understanding of the process of loss, grief, anger, guilt and resulting depression in childhood may aid us to help such children develop the resiliency and coping skills which they need in order to thrive in their families, in schools, and in society at large.

Chapter 12

FREEDOM AND DIRECTION: RECIPE FOR A GOLDEN AGE

A s adults, when we think back to the best parts of being a kid, we tend
to think of those middle years when summer days passed in a golden
haze of playing involved games which ended only with dusk and being
called in, reluctantly, by mothers on porches; we remember best friends
and secret pacts and reading under the covers at night, years punctuated
by birthdays, school vacations and family trips; we remember new outfits
for the first day of school, and having everyone's favorite—or least
favorite—teacher for a whole year, and the agonizing wait to find out if
someone sent a valentine to us in the box at the front of the classroom.
Probably most of us think of those days as the real crux of childhood—
somehow enchanted and special—when we were old enough to do some
exciting things, but too young to have to think much about the future. As
with most other memories of the past, these are selective: we don't tend
to remember the doubts and fears, nights spent crying, days spent convinced we weren't good enough, times when our little sister got a better
present, our best friend betrayed us or our dog died. We remember the
real traumas and the golden haze, and not much in between.

But between the ages of six and nine, children undergo a series
of rapid and interrelated changes which may be both exciting and
bewildering. As they get used to spending more time outside their own
homes their relationships with their immediate and extended families
change, and they come to a clearer awareness of themselves within their
family. Leaving the familiarity of the home, children start to recognize
that adults who fill a variety of roles—teacher, hockey coach, brownie
leader, swim teacher, camp counsellor—may have different expectations
of them than did their families and may react differently to them as
people, and they learn that they must adjust their own behaviour
accordingly. As they enter a larger world, they have a greater freedom to
explore, to develop interests and friendships outside those of their

161

families, and to learn to adapt to new situations, people, and feelings. They are beginning the long, ten to fifteen year trek down the road, over the hill, and across the bridge to independent adulthood!

In normal development, then, a child passes through regular sequences based on the interaction of biological factors and experience. The child moves through successive levels of development, perhaps with some problems but nevertheless effectively, mastering demands at each level in order to move on to the next. He carries along the satisfactions and frustrations of each stage, and either his experiences help him develop effectively or leave him vulnerable and perhaps overpowered by the needs of an earlier developmental stage. His concerns and fears as he enters school can be countered by successes at an earlier age and he views himself as potentially capable. He knows there are parents, and by implication other adults, who will help when help is asked for, and he generally expects that he will be all right.

And, in a normal family, parents lay the foundation for their child's development from birth through their acceptance, care, and guidance; both freedom and direction are key components of the dynamics of such a family. They recognise and satisfy their children's feelings of both dependency and independence; they accept their children as individuals while helping them see that they are connected to others; they set limits which help children to understand safety needs, the needs of others, and the consequences of their own behavior; they accept and are expressive of feelings; they talk and listen, explore and learn, share and co-operate as a family; they teach survival skills for life in the larger world; they encourage a child's interests and the expression of his or her ideas and talents; they are warm, firm, supportive, fair, predictable, child-focused: most of the time they enjoy their children! Over the pre-school years, they help a child to feel trusted, loved, accepted—an integral part of a family—as well as a self-confident and capable individual.

This chapter concerns itself with providing some guidelines for teachers and others who work with children who are not developing normally, emotionally and cognitively—specifically with overprotected and rejected children. Clearly just as normal children come from families which function positively, children with such problems come from families with more problematic dynamics at work. Such children develop lowered self-esteem which may be most noticeable in their attitudes toward learning and to authority and in difficulties developing positive peer relationships.

We will attempt to draw some informal "pictures," as an outside adult might see them. First, four normal children within this age range, who all might be products of the kind of family dynamics summarised above. Next we will look at the deviations and exaggerations of the normal behaviors expected as exhibited by an overprotected child and the family dynamics involved, and then those of a rejected child and the dynamics which produced such behavior. An understanding of the family dynamics involved is necessary for an adult who works with such children in order to avoid "playing in to" established patterns the child has with adults. Last, we will look at how a teacher, coach, group leader, camp counsellor or other adult who works with children might be able to adapt his or her own behaviour to help such a child be more successful, emotionally and cognitively, at adapting to life outside his or her own family.

Six-year-old Chris is expansive and undiscriminating, the centre of the world, who knows everything, wants everything and wants it his own way—now! He may act like a baby at times but, at others, he is surprisingly "grown up"—he may catch the exact inflection of an adult comment, or repeat overheard statements at inappropriate moments which make his parents cringe. His name is important to him; he likes to be called by his name and to write it on everything. He tries to do things on his own, even those patently un-do-able, and may resist help from others stubbornly. Chris has more energy than any adult, endless questions to ask, riddles and jokes to repeat—the same ones over and over—and he wants lots of positive adult attention for any and all of his achievements. Chris gets cuddled now only when he is willing to sit still for it, and can throw awesome temper tantrums when crossed!

At seven years old, Gina is more self conscious about her body than she was the year before. She fears things which threaten the identity she is comfortable with, and dislikes new situations, new people in her life, new clothes, having a haircut or being criticized and laughed at, even gently, by her friends or family. Gina needs adults to like her and she wants to know her place in the world, but she has very few ways of realistically evaluating her progress. She is apt to expect too much from herself and then feel inadequate; she is more likely to be on the sidelines than taking the risks she might have taken a year previously, whether in a game, telling a joke for adults, or in a class. She can chatter for hours with a trusted friend or adult, and tell elaborate stories with lots of magic and fantasy involved. Gina likes to "own" her favourite people, and can sulk really well when she can't have as much of their time and attention as she wants!

Now he is eight, Billy is more outgoing and aware of experiences, more critical both of things around him and of himself. He hates injustice, perceived or real, whether his sister's larger helping of dessert or someone picking on a smaller child. He tries to live up to the standards of others and feels guilt or shame if he doesn't think he is doing so. Success in school is thus important, because the mark or grade means that he has an evaluation and can judge himself by it. Unfortunately, if marks are low, he may see himself as unable to do things and may prove it by successive failures, or by not attempting something he thinks he can't master. He likes belonging to a small, cohesive group, usually made up only of boys, with endless hours of active games with rules, and he always plays to win. He's capable of great loyalty to friends and to the succession of heroes, usually athletes, with whose success he identifies. If Billy's not outside playing with his friends, or watching TV, he's probably asleep. But he only seems to be leading life totally externally!

Ellen at 9 is concerned with doing things well because competence, mastery, and industry help her to be, and feel, more independent. She feels in charge of her body, and may like gymnastics or dance or other activities which let her display the effects of practise and hard work. Ellen likes secrets and rituals, craft work, pen pals, animal stories, a tidy bedroom, working for badges in Guides, taking care of—or bossing around—younger children. She is less dependent on others and takes pride in showing better impulse control, in being "good" at school. She is very competitive within her group of girlfriends, and can play endless games, many quite complicated or based on tricking someone—card and board games are favourites. She accepts rules and laws, and can be quite critical of adults she sees as breaking them. She talks articulately, argues well, and has a firm grasp of what she feels ought to be happening in a classroom or group or family; she likes organizing things and people, and by so doing makes them predictable. Ellen can be pretty self-righteous at this age!

* * * *

In the intense atmosphere of her overprotective home, where she is loved or admired not for herself but for her accomplishments, eight year old Theresa quickly got the message, "as long as I produce I am loved." She feels she must produce more and more to maintain her parents' love, without knowing what would happen if she stopped fulfilling their expectations. She has been raised not to ask questions or talk back, and can easily be made to feel very guilty for real or imagined transgressions against unspoken family codes. She seldom is allowed to go places besides those her parents have chosen, or to bring friends home to play, so Theresa plays alone a good deal, often with her large family of dolls, who talk more and have more exciting lives than she does. She is very neat, a perfectionist who does her homework carefully but with little imagination, seems uncomfortable in groups of children and tends to hover near her mother if the family goes out together. She is highly self-conscious, almost prim, about her body and its functions, and tends to be a bit of a hypochondriac, which is encouraged by her mother. She misses a lot of school and doesn't participate in any after school activities. She is nice, quiet, obedient, doesn't make messes or take risks—she seems always to be holding her breath anxiously; Theresa doesn't ever seem to really laugh out loud or enjoy herself.

Overprotective families such as Theresa's encourage dependency and discourage any independent actions in their children. They are not very flexible in terms of rules and expectations, and tend to be pessimistic about the world; conservative themselves, they encourage docile, passive acceptance and conformity in their children. They value neatness, obedience, good manners, a regular schedule; they reward academic achievement and prefer it to be in areas where there are "right" answers; they tend to not allow children to be involved in active peer groups, or to encourage music, art, drama or anything else which seems imaginative rather than practical. They tend to stifle and smother feelings, to control children through guilt and to not allow aggression or even verbal anger; observed physical affection in such families often seems mechanical rather than an expression of spontaneous feeling.

Such overprotective families regulate and watch over every physical detail of their children's lives long after it is unnecessary—amounts eaten, hours slept, teeth brushed, bowel movements, clothing selected—and encourage physical dependency, often including hypochondria; minor injuries and sore throats may result in much coddling which allows the parents to control children's activities as they could when they were still infants. They tend not to have close relationships outside the family, and actively discourage such relationships for their children—there is a very in-bred atmosphere, in which the real world seems not to matter much. It is not infrequent to find such kids have never slept overnight at someone else's house, or gone to an adventurous birthday party, or to camp, or on school trips where dirt/risk/noise may be involved. Children from such families frequently are seen as depressed and lonely by outside adults, and seem to be at higher risk for suicide, anorexia, and bulimia in adolescence.

* * * *

Brian has experienced rejection all his life from his parents, and learned very early that he couldn't rely on an adult. He was left to cry it out alone as an infant because "it will teach him to rely on himself." When he reached up for a hug, he was ignored because his mother was "too busy"; when he fell and hurt himself, he was told "it doesn't *really* hurt"; if he complained of an injustice, he was called "a crybaby"; if he needed help doing something, he was rebuffed with "you're old enough to do that by yourself"; if he made a mistake, he was "stupid." If a neighbor or teacher complained, his parents might— or might not, he could never be sure—stick up for him with the out- sider, but they could be counted on to assume he was guilty and to punish him harshly when the family was alone. When Brian needed to be fed, even as a small child, his parents would feed him on condition that he clean up his room. Because there is no relation between being fed and cleaning up the room, the message Brian heard was "if you do this for me, I'll do that for you; if you don't, don't expect anything from me either."

So Brian, at nine, tends to do things for himself whenever possible and not to trust or rely on adults; he seems old and bitter beyond his years. He is aloof, alienated, moody, suspicious and a loner, occasionally a bully; he seldom picks on anyone who might fight back, but specializes in intimidation. In class he dawdles, almost daring an adult to confront him; he sits at the back by himself and does little work to hand in, although he may in fact be bright, which might show up only on a test. He talks little, refuses to participate in group work kinds of projects, and seems immune to positive reinforcement. He has one or two older boys, much like him, as friends, but this is pretty much a "hanging around getting into trouble" group, with little shared conversation or fun. He likes physically aggressive sports, and could channel a lot of extra energy into them, but because he isn't a good team player he isn't welcomed by other kids in such games. He has no concept of sportsmanship and will kick someone when they're already down or humiliate someone if given a chance; Brian isn't playing a game, he's playing out his life, and he gives no quarter. Brian wears a perpetual sneer, a chip on his shoulder the size of the Canadian shield, and is totally wrapped up in an "I don't care—so what're you gonna do about it?" attitude toward the whole world; the only living creature he trusts or cares about is his dog, Pancho.

A family such as Brian's discourages emotional dependency and any kind of interpersonal interactions with its children. It encourages children to be prematurely selfreliant in unnecessary ways—propping up bottles for month-old infants rather than holding them, requiring children to make their own beds at two, take care of themselves after school at five, and so forth. The family is non-nurturing, seemingly totally uninterested in any of the child's physical or emotional needs. They seem to see children as interlopers, manipulators even as infants, claimants for too-rare resources to be battled against as if they were adults. The world is a "you scratch my back I'll scratch yours" place, and everyone's motives are suspect; there is more than a touch of paranoia in their feelings about others, especially schools and government agencies, and they tend to hold grudges forever, to be suspicious of offers of help or advice, even from long-time neighbors. They tend to be secretive and non-communicative as well as physically and verbally unaffectionate; physical relationships are likely to be casually if not actively violent-shove, push, pull, slap, kick.

Such a family is often rigid and inflexible in its demands of its children, but these demands have little to do with reality or with the child's capabilities—"if you flunk that test you're grounded for a month" may be a threat, although no encouragement to do well in school, and no help with homework, has preceded this threat. The sense is that the family is affronted if an outsider criticizes in some way—a teacher calling home about poor behavior, or absenteeism, or failing to do well, for example—and will punish the offender because of the complaint rather than the original behavior which prompted it. Often the family invokes authority, and expects instantaneous obedience to it, while hostile to any higher, outside authority, such as the police or a truant officer. Such families rarely voluntarily seek help for themselves or their children, or allow their children to talk about life in the family outside it. Children from such families are seen as chronically hostile by outsiders, and in adolescence tend to act out in a variety of anti-social ways; they are often prime candidates for substance abuse.

* * * *

Every experienced teacher has seen Theresa and Brian, or a variation of them, many times; on the first day of school it is with a sense of dismay—their reputations generally precede them in schools. After that it is likely to become more active—spiralling from frustration to attempted indifference to active dislike. And, sadly, the teacher's response is often withdrawal of attention or affection, isolation, sarcasm, rejection, or active hostility—none of which will help, all of which will simply reinforce for the child the patterns of interactions with adults which he or she has already mastered. Often teachers KNOW that what they are doing is not working, and dislike themselves for not being more patient, more therapeutic, more professional, but they are stymied by the behaviour of such children. What goes wrong between such a child and the teacher, and why is the relationship so predictable and, often, so rapidly established?

Let's look more closely at what we might see in the classroom.

Theresa is the quiet, obedient one who tries to become "teacher's pet"—to once again be smothered and protected, this time by the teacher rather than her mother. No negative feelings or behaviors are expressed, and the teacher has a quiet, hard working, perfectionistic child who needs or craves for protective covering. Even when she doesn't understand a new idea, she will quietly and smilingly accept it, and can give isolated bits back on demand, but is not usually able to integrate it into a body of knowledge without the teacher's direct help. She will ask for help so that the teacher will do things for her, show her again, but is so easily overwhelmed by information that she may be unable to use the help given. Theresa is so busy looking for cues about what the teacher wants her to do that she often doesn't attend to the actual information presented. Her language skills tend to be poor, partly because she has had little practice in actually communicating, partly because the independence implied by talking aloud what she thinks is too threatening. Almost anything that would require Theresa to compare, analyse, judge, or criticise is nearly impossible, because cognitively these are dangerous activities for her—they might lessen her dependency on adult decision making, and so they are avoided or denied.

If Theresa feels she is not doing well or that the teacher might not like her enough, she quickly tries to make reparation. She gives unasked-for little gifts, tries to do classroom clean up tasks to help out, stays in from recess or after school, hangs around the teacher's desk, all the while waiting wordlessly like a cocker spaniel for a pat on the head. The teacher cannot understand why this behavior is happening, since it was not caused by any real fault on Theresa's part, so often she is impatient, feels guilty for the impatience, and is made uncomfortable by what she sees as an inappropriate need, or immature, babyish behaviour.

As a result, she tries to push Theresa toward greater independence by ignoring her demands for affirmation and attention of the sort she is used to at home, or by pushing her toward a peer group which doesn't want her and in which she has no idea of how to function. This results in depression that reduces the quality and quantity of work, making her feel she is now unworthy and unacceptable, and has somehow been a bad child. She begins to under-achieve or fail at school work, or at gym; she cries a lot, is withdrawn, and becomes the butt of jokes. Essentially, she is a depressed child in need of help.

But, as Morris (1978) indicates, the efforts on the part of the school to help such children frequently increase or reinforce the child's sense of isolation. The child is removed for special help to remediate the academic or social problems, which further separates her from her peers, and tends to be helped on a one to one basis, which exacerbates the sort of dependency on a single adult for affirmation which has led to the depression in the first place.

At school Brian can see only another adult authority, which is a potential threat, as it suggests more organized manipulation to come. He is told there are rules which he must obey; he sees the rules as adult-made, not taking him into consideration, and searches for ways to defy or subvert them. He assumes the hostility of adults, and presents himself accordingly; he is remarkably successful at soliciting defensive behaviour in teachers as a result! His perpetual sneer drives away other kids, who assume he is judging them negatively. But Brian seldom recognizes how his actions make others feel, because his sensitivity, empathy and capacity for considering other people are all poor.

Brian, although the teacher may not see it, eagerly seeks out new information, but often once he has it, he feels it might be dangerous, because trying to use it might show him to be inadequate, so he generally attempts to hide what he does and doesn't know. He has a high drive for mastery, because his survival so far has been based on figuring out what adults might demand next, but he often doesn't take in enough to really understand, so that he operates at a very concrete level. He requires a lot of practice to really master information, but has a hard time settling down to repeat something often enough to do so, and thus forgets as quickly as he initially seemed to learn something. He tends to present his accomplishment or his answer over and over, with a lot of motor activity, as if he's afraid it will disappear.

Because he needs to make his pattern of decision for action or thinking independent of teacher directions, he has a hard time knowing how to utilise information. Scanning a concept is difficult for him, and he can only try one hypothesis at a time; his choices are often limited by his need to select what will give an immediate reward of the kind he has learned to value most. His language output is scanty and unimaginative because he has little to talk about—his environment and experiences have been limited, and communication within the family rare. He sees talking as a form of controlling behaviour, so may initiate conversations if he feels secure about a topic, but will usually not respond to other's questions or volunteer information in a general discussion.

Underneath, Brian needs to be close to an adult but is so afraid of letting down his guard and being hurt that he holds back. He may consciously only be able to think it through in terms of his experiences within his family: "If I got close to my teacher and liked her, she would be able to manipulate me, so I won't allow any closeness, kindness or warmth between us." Praise or rewards, which are involving, are shunned; marks, which are impersonal, can be accepted. Especially marks on things like math and spelling tests, where answers are clearly right, so the teacher can't possibly be trying to put one over on him. The child is looking for a machine or computer with no feelings, which cannot hurt him or find out what he doesn't know, and how much he desires closeness and warmth. If his marks are not high, he simply says "it doesn't matter" or, "if I worked I could get high marks" or "high marks are for sissies." He becomes aggressive in class to compensate for a lack of high marks and to prove he is dominant and needs no one. His behaviour often challenges other boys, whose own behavior worsens as they try, usually unsuccessfully, for his approval.

Paradoxically, his aggressive behaviour has the effect of forcing adults to try to control him, in an often escalating battle of wills, especially if there is a male teacher involved. Generally expulsion from the classroom to the office follows, but children like Brian perceive this as victory—they manipulated the teacher into responding in a very predictable way, and often the teacher lost his temper in the process and lost face with the rest of the class, although the teacher may not realize this. And, removed from the classroom, the teacher's only hope of involving such a child positively, through repeated small doses of academic success, is lost as well.

An awareness of the influence of early experiences on learning can prevent errors in judgment in the classroom which compound the child's problems at this crucial stage of learning and may have lifelong effects. Instead of labelling the overprotected child "learning disabled" in the best modern way, or writing off the rejected child as the traditional academic "hard nut to crack," teachers must understand that the difficulties of both are based on deeply ingrained emotional "survival skills" which are automatically brought to the classroom and reflected in the child's cognitive style as well as in relationships with both peers and adults. Her job then is to devise teaching methods which can make adjustments for these ingrained patterns which impede or distort the child's emotional, social, and academic development.

In attempting to develop curricula and teaching techniques which provide the richest possible learning experience for all children in the crucial early years at school, we need to concentrate on the particularly delicate balance between freedom and direction required in this period of rapid change and adjustment. On the one hand, children, full of their own physical energy and exhilarated by their growing awareness of their own powers as a person, naturally want to be doing. The teacher has to understand that it is difficult for them to sit still, and that neurologically they may not be prepared to work for long periods of time. The teacher must provide children with opportunity to be spontaneous, as this is their natural way of taking the world, of growing and learning. *Freedom*.

On the other hand, in trying to make sense for themselves out of the wealth of new experiences and perceptions provided by his own development and the changing environment, the child feels a strong need for direction. There is a need for routine, for regularity, for dependability, for consistency, in the teacher's attitude, and for reasonable limitations and criticism to help the child identify appropriate behaviour and conduct and to guide and focus his expanding powers. *Direction*.

In adjusting for these basic needs teachers must of course respect children's equally strong needs for warmth, acceptance and encouragement, as well as the individual child's particular level of development, cognitive style, and emotional characteristics. It is as unwise to expect 10-year-old behaviour from a child of 6 as it is to "free" a timid, overprotected child from all expectations and direction, or to expect a hostile, rejected child to work quietly with others from his first day at school. The basic aim of teachers must be to enable all children to develop a sense of worthiness which helps them overcome fears and difficulties while expressing aggressive energies in creative ways rather than in mere defiance of authority.

The most fruitful learning situation for both normal and maladjusted children at this stage is one which gives them the opportunity to become involved in the important work of play. A play-based program responds directly to the child's need for the freest possible body movement in order to explore his still-developing physical powers. Through play, the child not only refines his motor skills, but also develops adjustments of vision and control of speech and sound. Dramatic play also provides a core for the child's social, emotional, aesthetic and intellectual develop-ment, organizing different aspects of experience into wholes, opening up new insights and extending learning in the most natural way possible.

As Bruner (1973) said, "Play during early childhood permits the child to explore combinations of things and acts that would never be explored if he kept just to reasonable problem solving. It is for this reason that we can properly speak of play as the serious business of childhood."

In the physical area, play allows for body control and for sensori-motor skills development. As children can handle and control equipment, they do so with satisfaction and acquire competence which helps them feel good about themselves. The sensory experiences of exploring the world—its size, shape, weight, distance, speed, light—allow them to deal with concrete, tangible objects in their way, and through verbal imita-tions of two dimensional representations. Play at sensory motor experi-ences lets them investigate the "hard realities" of the world.

In the social area, children play with each other and learn how to inter-act. Their activity evolves from solitary play through to spectator play, to parallel play, associative play, and group play. Children learn to respond to each other's experiences, but at their own level of emotional growth. They are stimulated by the interactive experiences. Children imitate in play; co-operative behaviour emerges and children begin to accept in-struction. They learn to evaluate their activities honestly and not entirely egocentrically, and see how their behaviour and that of others affect them. They learn to postpone gratification and to recognize that they do not know everything. Until they can do this, they cannot actually learn from teachers. The child moves freely in and out of situations, advances and regresses, learns and recovers; social adjustment arises from within the child and is not a mere technique imposed from without.

Through dramatic play children learn to improvise possible solutions, share ideas, plan and structure actions, change endings or characters to satisfy the group's needs for form, deal with subjects which are both realistic and fantastic, make inferences and come to some conclusions about events around them, explore a variety of adult roles and reactions, and gain a sense of the range of human emotions and needs. They practise levels and styles of speech in improvised dialogue which build communication skills and enrich their sense of the power and joy of language.

For children whose early experiences have deprived them of the emotional foundations for learning, the opportunities in the classroom for play of all kinds will be crucial in helping them develop the schemata for acquiring knowledge. At the same time, the play itself also provides an important opportunity for the teacher to recognize, evaluate and make adjustments for the particular problems, abilities, and learning styles of individual children.

And for them, as for normal children, the wholeness and immediacy of play intensify the sensory experience and provide a natural opportunity for the symbolic expression which fosters aesthetic and linguistic development. Involved in play, the child feels the rhythm of body movement—gliding from a rope tied to a tree, climbing a staircase; she sees and feels the colour, form and texture of things—playing with sand, she feels its coolness and loose, dry quality, hears its scraping sound as she digs or its wooshing rush down a slide. Intent on organizing his wild animal hunt or store, he counts, imitates grown-up talk, and tells others what to do. When involved in a drama or telling a story or painting a picture or working with clay, she may reveal new verbal and symbolic resources to herself as well as to the teacher.

By offering children the opportunity to play with assorted materials and to evolve new and appropriate ways of making use of them in response to sensitive observation of what the play itself reveals, teachers can help children direct and organize a wealth of new experience and information for themselves. By involving the whole child, play facilitates the cognitive growth which, in the final reckoning, must come from within.

Freedom and direction, provided in balance by caring adults, can make it possible for all children to truly experience the middle years of childhood as the golden age we like best to remember it was for us.

Chapter 13

IF LOVE IS NOT ENOUGH, WHAT IS?
(WITH APOLOGIES TO BRUNO BETTELHEIM!)

Once upon a time, not so very long ago, the trend in North America was to remove a troubled child or adolescent from his familiar class in school and place him in a "special" classroom of some sort in the same school; when that failed to produce the desired results, the child might be moved to a special ed class in a different school, outside his own neighborhood; when this too failed, the child might be moved to a foster home or a group home, and finally, if these did not work, the last placement before the system admitted defeat was an institution, generally well removed from his own community and family. After two or three years of treatment, the child would be sent home again. And far too often he could not remain there, because his problems reappeared and could not be handled by the family.

In our hurry to remove children from what we perceived to be unwholesome settings at home or in school, we failed to take into account what such separation meant, emotionally, to the child and to his or her family. Slowly we began to try to work with families and children at the same time and to try to prepare them for the eventual homecoming. Sometimes it worked, too often it didn't. Too many times children were left, psychologically, with such an impaired sense of membership in their biological family when they came out of treatment centres or training schools at sixteen, that they ended up living on their own in rooming houses—too often unschooled and unskilled—with few people available in their network of emotional support who could be sufficiently helpful as they tried to live adult lives in a complex society. Children and families alike felt abused by a system which, however, was an attempt to do "the best thing" for all concerned.

The recognition came slowly that institutionalization was only appropriate when and if no other help was possible and in cases where the child was a real danger to him or herself or to family and community.

175

The move to take treatment of children back into the ordinary classroom, the neighborhood, the family, has gained momentum over the years. As we all know, there has been much opposition to group homes in many communities and even to the provision of special education, not in enclosed settings but in neighborhood schools, in many school districts. People often do not want to "see" the troubled child in their midst, especially next door or at the desk next to their child in school.

These children seem to give many people an uncomfortable feeling, perhaps because they are a threat to the omnipotence that most adults feel and think they possess in relation to children—since children are small, they should be controllable by adults. But here we have children who are not responding to adult ministrations and that makes us feel inadequate. It also makes us feel guilty: we are failing with these children and we don't want to see our failures. It's just too threatening. And so we put them in institutions, usually at the outskirts of a city or in a rural area—with the inane rationalization that fresh air will be therapeutic!

Both the children and the families have difficulty coping with these moves and separations. Important events occur in each of their lives which are not witnessed by the other, and their lives begin to move slowly away from each other. You might compare this to the "best friends" of childhood who drift apart, and when reunited, can only talk about the communal past, relive the "good old days." Except in this instance disturbed children and their families, when brought together after years apart, often have only bittersweet memories to share. They no longer have common experiences to talk about, and have lost the feeling of belonging because they have been forcibly separated by a system which has failed them. Unfortunately the lack of common experiences for two or three years makes reconciliation or return difficult, if not impossible.

Another comparison might be to the severed lives of children who live with one parent after a divorce and cannot see the other parent more than occasionally over the years; although they may have many good memories, they grow out of practise about how to relate to each other. The games and outings which marked their early weekends or vacations together are no longer appropriate, but they have no other model with which to work. Their discomfort at this is heightened by the sense that they "ought" to know each other well, be close, be comfortable, since they are parent and child. Although such a separation is not as traumatic, usually, as the institutionalization of a child, both have repercussions for the child's adjustment in adulthood and for his or her own eventual parenting.

Clearly as the years have passed we have come to recognize the inherent dangers in the separation of parents and children, the splitting of families, even when children are emotionally at risk or damaged by the family conditions. Even in cases where long term professional help is clearly indicated, or a child needs to be separated from his or her family for reasons of physical safety, the gap between the time a child is tested, or referred to an agency, or sent by a judge, and the time space becomes available in a group home or institution is often lengthy. Too often the reliance on eventual institutionalization has discouraged the provision of interim treatment; sometimes by the time there is space, a child can no longer be successfully treated, and may be on the streets somewhere.

At the same time as we realized the limitations of institutionalization, and perhaps luckily, the funding for the very expensive treatment centres and training schools dried up. It would be comforting if one could think that a recognition of the usual recidivism rate, the inability of most disturbed children to function as stable adults after leaving such institutions, and the damages caused by such separations to children and families, were the causes of the cutbacks, but clearly this was not the case. Political expediency and increasing demands by groups which were represented by larger numbers within the population generally accounted for such budgetary cutbacks.

At the same time as budgets for facilities were being cut, the identification of more and more children in need of alternative help snowballed. Problem children were delegated instead to a wide variety of social service agencies, and as such agencies multiplied, we found that troubled children in ordinary classrooms were being increasingly referred for help. In addition to the children who had formerly been seen as needing institutional help—the acutely physically handicapped or emotionally disturbed—whole new categories grew up into which troubled children could be slotted. Such children were labelled as hyperactive, distractible, minimally brain damaged, learning disabled, aggressive, underachieving, withdrawn—and were sent outside the school system, usually without sufficient diagnoses and/or remedies being applied within the classroom first.

In our zeal to treat children—or in our zeal to remove children who created some fuss, or required individualized methods, or took up too much teacher or parent time—we lost sight of the fact that many children go through stages of boisterousness, clannish behaviour, hyperactivity, aloneness, lack of interest in schoolwork, and a myriad of other behaviours which became part of "packages" of symptoms for these new ailments. We didn't look very carefully at the research or information about child development—rather if we thought we saw a problem, we packed the child off to the nearest agency. Sending one's child for some kind of "learning" help—a tutor, a learning centre, a therapist—became almost as essential to middle class life as the inevitable braces and "educational" summer camps and lessons, with the resulting proliferation of not only public agencies, but private businesses and schools set up to educate or treat children who may or may not have been particularly carefully evaluated or diagnosed.

So as a result of some very sound reasons—the ineffectiveness of most institutionalization, financial pressures felt by government funding agencies, increasing numbers of middle class referrals, and the acute pressures on families in inner city areas and resultant behavioral and emotional difficulties in their children—alternatives to institutionalization have been strenuously sought. The reality is that there are not enough services for children and families in trouble anywhere today. Even if one assumed that every special education class, group foster home, treatment centre, private school for children with learning disabilities, psychologist, social worker, teacher, child care worker and psychiatrist in North America were excellent and perfectly able to devise sound treatment plans based on careful diagnosis, all of them, working full steam ahead, twelve hours a day, seven days a week for decades could not *begin* to cope with the number of children and families in need, or who are said to be in need, of service.

One has only to listen to social workers at children's agencies, inner city teachers, or psychologists, to recognize that overwork is the reality for all of them, with the real danger of subsequent burnout which so often follows such a load. Long term individual psychotherapy has become a item which is often only possible if one tries to ignore the long waiting lists and the thousands of children who receive no help while one fortunate child is being treated. Our guess is that for every child who receives the treatment he or she needs there are four others today who are treated inappropriately, insufficiently, or not at all.

It is clear, then, that the search for sound therapeutic alternatives must be an important priority for all those seriously concerned with the mental health of the children in this complex and chaotic society in which we live. It would be too easy, however, to begin trying all sorts of different, currently trendy alternatives randomly. As in education, there are always fashionable new directions in therapy which may not bear close scrutiny. We firmly believe that the psychological diagnosis of the individual child must be the place at which the building of alternative strategies begins. Just as no miracle drug cures every physical illness, no miracle therapy works for every child. Treatment in the dark, "winging it" so to speak, or the therapist who "does it how it feels right today" is ultimately very destructive. Beware also of the therapist who has a pet "method" which he or she swears can help any child.

If treatment is to be useful, it must begin with a detailed picture of the core issues of the child's problems. Knowing a child's specific difficulties in many different areas of functioning, and recognizing the kind of pattern the acting out or symptoms indicate, help us to formulate treatment goals which are particular to that child. The family involvement and problems and the child's key relationships tell us what to try to treat, what not to touch, which family members to see, how often, and with what goals in mind. We have to recognize the limitations within us, within the family, and within the child.

We cannot realistically hope to change all the relationship patterns of a family—often twenty years in the making at least—which impinge on the child's existence. Nor can we hope to have much impact on a particular school or community or on traditional ethnic group patterns of socialization. Sometimes the old maxim about having the wisdom to recognize what we can change and what we cannot seems particularly apt. There are many times when we have realized that a troubled adolescent stuck in a family which has no desire to change, needs to develop the strength to endure and gain some understanding of why his or her family is the way it is, so that he or she can tolerate more, and hate less, until it is time to leave home.

Every adolescent must have the opportunity to become involved in a process effective for him or her, even if the parents do not agree or cooperate. In such a case the process would be one of helping him or her to recognize some of the dynamic relationships within the family, how individual troubles may be an expression of resentment toward the family, and in some cases how the adolescent may have been selected unconsciously to be the bearer of the family pathology.

Equally important, especially with adolescents, is the need for the individual to feel competent and be seen as an achieving member of his peer group. Mastery and competence at some skill, or in some area, are as important to many troubled adolescents as psychotherapy, particularly when the family insists on not being involved. It is difficult to help an adolescent when his family isn't there to stand beside him, and thus for many adolescents group therapy is far more useful. Within a therapy group made up of peers, the adolescent is able to be, and as importantly, to feel, useful to his or her peers and thus eventually comes to see him or herself as a true partner in the therapeutic process. The bonds knit between peers in such groups often go far beyond the active treatment time of the group itself and provide an enormously valuable safety net.

We have developed over the years a classification system in an attempt to simplify the traditional system of diagnosis and to enable us to think of problems as treatable rather than intractable. If we talk about "personality disorders" or "schizophrenia," those terms have such a heavy connotative loading that we may in fact be predisposed to feel that treatment cannot be successful. One theoretical position suggests that we must await further advances in genetics and biochemistry for some solutions to personality disorders and the schizophrenias. This model suggests that those psychological problems may be created by hormonal, organic and genetic dysfunctions and need further examination and experimentation to develop adequate treatment systems. This may be the case; but there is also sufficient reason to believe that biochemical, organic, or genetic factors can be viewed as stimuli which set in motion a series of other events which may culminate in such disorders.

We suggest that instead of viewing the organic picture as a closed system, we regard it as a system of successive variables which trigger events within the familial system and which disrupt the psychological satisfactions at several developmental levels. No matter whether the initial stimulus is psychological, genetic, or biochemical, the response to the behaviour exhibited by the child will be exaggerated or made less dominant depending on how people in the child's environment respond.

Children's behavioral characteristics result from the interaction between them and their immediate environment—usually family. Our way to think about problems is to describe children's personalities in terms of "behavioural organizational strategies," that is, the way they do things, and the balance between imagination and reality. What separates the normal child from one who is seriously disturbed is often the degree and the amount of the child's ego strength. It is this, and the child's capacity to maintain internal integration in the face of change and stress, which allow us to talk of the child's personality as being normal or outside of the normal range. Ego strength determines the child's capacity to handle and work through situations rather than develop symptoms (Weininger, 1986).

Once a careful diagnosis has been made and the needs of the child are clearly defined, the search for a treatment method can be safely undertaken. Obviously we never like to be in the position of having to say, "well, this child needs long term individual psychotherapy but due to time/financial/ caseload reasons we will just have to substitute three group therapy sessions." Unfortunately that is all too often the case. Instead of wasting time and energy bemoaning this reality, we think we should focus on the development of a whole range of alternatives which the mental health profession can realistically hope to deliver. The wider the variety of possible choices, the more likely we are to be able to find one which is both psychologically appropriate and pragmatically possible to achieve. The alternatives put forward now reflect our experiences and, of course, our biases about the nature of successful therapy.

An interesting study done in 1978 by a colleague of Dr. Weininger's, Mary Morris, involves using a teacher-consultant methodology to help identify depressed children within ordinary classrooms, and then to try to change the relationships these children had with the classroom teacher by working with the teacher. Although this study dealt with a small number of children, the process worked well with children who had been suffering from depression for at least two years and who were, at the point of the study, failing both academically and socially. Both observations and traditional instruments of evaluation were used to measure depression in these children. The consultant worked with the teachers with the aim of exploring and relieving problems in the teacher-pupil relationship. The consultant saw each child only for the initial screening work; all subsequent work was done by the teacher.

The teachers had found that the depressive features in children created considerable difficulties for them and " . . . almost all teachers were concerned that their approaches to the depressed child might be hurtful. They seemed to experience their approaches as intrusions into the child's withdrawn state which would "shatter" the child, as if a special fragility were present. Such fears about relating to the depressed child (along with a special concern and desire to help the child) created varying degrees of ambivalence for most teachers which seemed to inhibit their relationship to the depressed child" (Morris, 1978).

At the end of the study significant positive change was measured with the depressed children, with increased frequency of interactions and effective dependency on the teacher. In addition, teachers reported they enjoyed more, and had less frustration working with, depressed children. Their peers became more involved with the depressed children as well. Morris felt that these changes resulted from the combination of dependency-facilitating processes in the classroom, personality factors in the children, such as an openness to respond to such processes, and the procedures used in the study, i.e., consultation with the teachers which had mobilized them to become less frightened of harming the depressed children, more available to them for support, and having a greater understanding of their own reactions to such children.

Thus teacher consultation is one alternative in helping problem children in the classroom. It seems most feasible when the complex of symptoms is fairly easy to recognize and a highly specialized level of training is not necessary. Certainly it enables one to work with a larger number of children who need help than does direct psychotherapy.

A second alternative which does not involve enormous commitment of therapist time is the development of "kitchen nurseries" for physically handicapped children. Many children who need not be institutionalized for physical reasons nonetheless go through this process for practical reasons: their families lack the facilities to care for them at home, the province pays for their care in an institution but is much less helpful to children who could be living at home provided help was available, their families fear they cannot handle the 24 hour a day routine of physical care, and so forth. If fairly local arrangements could be made to bring such children together for half a day, everyday, either at someone's house or in a nursery type facility so that the children could develop peer relationships with others who share their problems, and relief and instruction could be provided for their families, then many children could be spared the enormous psychological damage likely to result from long term hospitalization.

Another alternative which does not require taking children away from their families and communities is a place such as the Madison Avenue School Project in Toronto. This school was designed as a long-term research project to help children with serious emotional disturbances — some with possible cerebral damage — and for children and adolescents who got into trouble with the law, as well as children who had developed emotional disturbances along with learning disabilities. An important component of this school was providing support for children's families in order to make it possible for them to continue to live with their children in spite of the enormous stress involved.

This school worked because we had some clear principles by which we were operating. We intended to create a milieu conducive to learning, with an emphasis on interpersonal relationships. Strictly academic subjects were seen as only part of the total learning experience of the child; play projects were developed individually by the staff for each child. We were prepared to teach the whole child, taking into account all the problems he brought to the school with him, and to integrate all learning experience for him. This did not mean a permissive environment but rather one in which we recognized the individual strengths and weaknesses of our children. This was possible to a large degree because each teacher worked only with a very few children at a time, frequently on a one-to-one or small group basis.

Traditionally small special education classes have fostered this kind of close and nurturing emotional relationship, but unfortunately they have too often been hampered by lack of knowledge about how and in what direction to proceed to ensure academic as well as emotional growth. The teachers of these classes are also under the "in school" pressure to have their classrooms and children look "normal," and the structure of the public school system has often actively discouraged such teachers from trying to work closely with the family and with whatever resources are available for the child in the community. At the Madison Avenue School these strictures didn't exist and thus an overall support system could be carefully built and maintained for each child. Those children from the Madison Avenue School who returned to public schools usually went back at their appropriate grade level with no need for unusual academic remediation in the scholastic sense. Learning goes on if the milieu is conducive to learning.

Family work was obviously necessary to our plans if the children were to remain at home with reasonable comfort for families and children alike, but family work started only when we could encourage the family to become involved in it. No unusual pressures were applied which might aggravate a child's already bad family situation, and as a result only two of the more than thirty-five children involved from 1971–79 were removed by their parents. This is notable because in a voluntary treatment program, parent hostility toward a child's improvement is not an unusual reaction: many children act as the container for their families' problems and act out the difficulties of the family by being sick/delinquent/ a school failure, etc. As the child improves and if the family has refused family or couple therapy, then usually the family begins to fall apart, for there is no one to absorb their hostilities and act out their problems so that they don't have to do so. Rather than become involved in therapy, and experience the anxiety of family reorganization, they remove the child from the situation in which he is getting better. Some of the guiding principles of this school were probably neither new nor original; by and large they were an extension of what takes place in a normal family (Weininger & Muskat, 1978).

We think that establishment of schools such as this one is an extremely important alternative. The response of many public school systems when approached for financial funding for such ventures is quite shortsighted; obviously the cost of working with a very low pupil-teacher ratio and a large number of support staff—psychologists, child care workers, and family workers—is higher when compared to ordinary elementary classrooms. But viewed as a financial alternative to the current cost of institutionalization, especially in light of the positive long term ramifications for both the child and the family, the cost is really very low. Every untreated child who becomes an unhappy and frustrated adult is likely to be unproductive for society as well as quite possible needing later societal support, financially, or eventual treatment help for him or herself or his or her children. The loss to society of well adjusted, stable, functioning adults is beyond estimation.

Another alternative is the community clinic setting, where a number of different kinds of therapies and resources can be available—individual psychotherapy, play therapy, group therapy, family therapy, child care workers working with a family for several months to teach new ways of interacting with each other—these are only some of the possibilities.

A clinic might also serve as a general focal point for the community; for example, an empty school building could easily become a valuable resource for all ages. A drop in centre for senior citizens, with hot meals and the use of shops and libraries, dental and medical care and help with financial or legal problems as well as a full range of recreational opportunities might make all the difference between the depressed and lonely old person living in a barren room who has to be institutionalized and the one who sees himself as a functioning, useful person. A day nursery could be provided, open 18 hours a day for parents working shifts, which might utilize seniors as "grandparents" to work with and read to their children. Daily or weekly play sessions could be held for immigrant children, with English language instruction scheduled at the same time, along with an informal, comfortable place for their mothers to meet; trips could be organized around the neighborhood to familiarize the newly arrived with the locations, names and purposes of their new neighborhood. Such a centre might also organize and staff camps which would not only give children and their parents a needed break from urban poverty or stress, but also allow each family member to make a visible contribution to the family's comfort. Learning and having fun together are a valuable "glue" for any family.

Guidance for new, young mothers could also be part of such a centre, especially for single parents and those living in poverty with practical sessions, on how to play with their children and care for them adequately, how to plan and prepare nutritious meals; use of the playground and nursery facilities would give them a break in the never-ending routine of child care, and allow them to meet new friends. Tutors to help those parents who, for some reason have had to drop out of school, either in organized classes or for helping individuals with correspondence courses, could be located in such a centre. After school recreational programs for children and evening sessions for parents on a variety of subjects could be offered as well.

Obviously these are not new ideas: Hull House, begun by Jane Adams in Chicago, and the settlement houses operated by social agencies and churches, especially in new immigrant areas, have been a major force in community work for decades. But there is no reason why such a network of services cannot be provided along with education, in the same location, for people of all ages, seven days a week—the community school concept with which many urban areas have already experimented. Shrinking enrollment in inner city areas gives us an unprecedented chance to do this, and the sense of loss which a community experiences when its school closes down would then be unnecessary.

Community centres such as this, combining social service agencies, recreation, mental health care, and schooling, are often *not* established primarily because of bureaucratic buck-passing and an inability of professionals to work together: each group is too interested in protecting its own "turf." Because of lack of active promotion and the complexity of organizing and funding them on the part of various departments within city, provincial or state, and federal governments, such clinics/centres are rare, and, once started, difficult to continue. The obvious dictum that an ounce of prevention is worth a pound of cure seems to go unnoticed in the treatment business!

The alternative with which Dr. Weininger has been most actively involved over the years is play psychotherapy. This is a fairly encompassing term; sometimes it refers to the technique of play analysis which is part of classic psychoanalytic work, sometimes to acting out family roles and conflicts in psychodrama, sometimes to more formalized techniques using dolls in situational poses to help elicit responses from a child which indicate feelings about his or her family. It can also mean a child's general release of tension and anxiety through a form of play with few limits set by the adults involved. And sometimes it means a type of non-directive, client-centered therapy which embodies some or all of the above approaches.

Not everyone could or should undergo play psychotherapy, and a child needs to have sufficient ego strength to endure the therapeutic relationship and to have had a sufficiently good primary relationship which was both consistent and long lasting. Many deprived children unfortunately lack one or both of these; in such cases the process must be adapted to the children. Some of the important changes I (Dr. Weininger) have made are to learn to use fewer words and to use specific play materials for their problems, rather than assuming that dolls or puppets or art materials are the only appropriate toys. For example, in working with an 11-year-old boy who had very little to say; he had been a witness to his father's attempt to kill his younger sister, and his mother had decided that she was a lesbian and had left the family. The child felt he had no one to be with and the symptoms he exhibited were aggression and fighting, demanding and impulsive behavior, failure in school, running away, and refusal to talk—along with an unusually strong fear of going to sleep. He had been with other therapists and nothing had happened, so he was used to failure and in fact expected it in relationships, not surprisingly under the circumstances.

In his first two sessions we were very quiet and spoke very little. He fidgeted and wanted to do something. Object relations theory (Weininger, 1984) indicates that at about this age boys are concerned with mastery and competence and need to feel control over their depressive feelings. I suggested we play seven card stud. Cards embody the "doing something," control is gained over the expression of aggression by using the card to say "I beat you" and "how stupid you are." But perhaps even more importantly, playing cards makes use of numbers, and the child was very interested in numbers, perhaps as an "anal," characteristic diagnosed in this child. The card game and its inherent qualities could be used by the child in a way which demonstrates his mastery and control over a fighting relationship while gaining satisfaction for certain psychological needs. He could add the numbers, decide he has enough to win, challenge the therapist, bluff, tease — all those things which in ordinary face to face talk he could not do. He could express his feelings through the indirectness of the card game and yet still experience the satisfactions which help him overcome his difficulties.

After several sessions he was more talkative, calm, co-operative and enthusiastic, and his behavior at home and school slowly improved. Obviously I don't feel that just playing cards with a disturbed child will turn his life around, but as a form of play psychotherapy appropriate to his age, home situation, and disturbance it was a good place to begin!

John Munn, a colleague, has used a table hockey game as a play psychotherapy tool. This was especially useful in working with verbal adolescent boys as a safe and contained method for expression of aggression, conflicts, resistances and defences, either directly or symbolically (Munn, 1978). Verbal communication with the therapist can be avoided and yet the process of playing with the game provides a rich source of content which can be interpreted directly to the child or indirectly through the players of the board, depending on the adolescent and the stage of treatment.

Besides the use of non-traditional toys or games, I have worked with mother-child dyads to help them to enjoy things together and to help mothers recognize the ways that their children respond to them. When they are able to see themselves as "good enough" mothers providing for their babies, then there are surprising changes in the mother-child relationship: the babies act positively to the mothers and the mothers return this positive affect (Winnicott, 1965).

I also use the telephone to help with some problems; in this way it is possible to create a dependency relationship and yet avoid a sense of inadequacy. Some individuals, because of their culture and/or experiences, need help but can not allow themselves to see a therapist. If forced to do so, the anxiety they experience is often more than the relationship can bear and they often leave feeling that they were wrong to come in the first place. The feeling that they can function with just the help of telephone conversations makes some people feel more able to accept help, especially in certain groups where seeking professional help, and taking off work to go, still has a profound stigma attached.

I have often written letters to adolescents and young people in penal institutions when they have the freedom to write what they wish. My letters are always on only one page, always relate to an aspect they talk about, and always offer an interpretation about which they can think. I try to talk to the unconscious and "bypass" the conscious, to satisfy unconscious needs with the intention that this will influence their conscious thoughts and actions.

Treatment forms such as psychodrama, music, art, dance and poetry therapies depend, as do all of the above, on the training of the therapist and the relationship of the therapist to the person. These, and those discussed above, all depend on intensive training, experience, and close supervision at the start if a therapist is going to be able to cope and to understand the very powerful processes of transference and countertransference (Weininger, 1984b, 1989). Throughout the late 60's and early 70's, the proliferation of group homes and treatment centres based on a philosophy of treatment, often worked out by a particular psychologist, psychiatrist, or social worker, missed this important point. A method worked out carefully by a knowledgeable therapist and applied to work with children by that person in appropriate circumstances and after careful diagnosis is not a guaranteed "cookbook for treatment" when used by well meaning but untrained others. Too often the assumption was that any compassionate but psychologically untrained young adult could apply such a method to every child encountered. However, the child often transfered elements from his or her relationships with absent parents to the new child care worker. This was very often a rapid process and one difficult for inexperienced workers to deal with; similarly, the countertransference of feelings left over from the worker's own childhood, set in motion by the hostility and acting out of the child, could result in some very destructive moments for both.

Treatment cannot be done by the seat of one's pants or on the basis of intuition alone. We have known one or two very good child care workers who said openly that they didn't want to confuse themselves by knowing too much about psychology because it might muddy their intuitive ability with kids; by and large they were strong and sensitive adults who were unaware that they knew more than they realized, and they came from stable families. But we certainly wouldn't consider this viewpoint as a desirable one from which to begin to work with children! We have also known some very well trained psychotherapists who do their students an injustice by implying that "you don't need intensive training in diagnosis and dynamics", and that you can "do it as it feels."

All this gives treatment a bad name, because treatment won't work if you don't know what you're doing. Perhaps one of the reasons why children's mental health work, along with education, has suffered such a drop in public confidence, and thus a drop in public financial support, is because during the years when trendy therapies abounded and treatment centres of many varieties sprang up, the public's expectations were unrealistically heightened. These therapies and places claimed to have the answers for disturbed children, as the schools of the sixties claimed to have the cure for society's ills through new and expensive facilities and methods. Ultimately both systems failed to deliver the expected "cure," due to similar lack of careful research and training, poor supervision of new methods, and not focusing on the child's needs. A certain skepticism, even cynicism, developed in the public mind about the value of psychology in general and therapy in particular.

The other crucial element in the provision of any form of treatment, whether for adults or children, traditional or new, individual or group, is the relationship of the individual to the therapist. We are convinced that there is no one "right" therapy and that, in fact, even if we found a method which seemed flexible enough to provide a possible use with many people, it could not apply to every individual, nor be used by every therapist. We don't think the best trained therapist in the world will succeed with a child he or she doesn't like; moreover, the most potentially treatable child will not respond to the therapist whose personality does not allow him or her to recognize the child's needs for play and activity. It is very difficult to predict a match between therapist and child, but it is possible to indicate that this particular child would work much better with a woman than a man, or that it is wisest to have a male and female therapist work together with a family, or that adolescents usually achieve much greater gains when they work in small groups with a well trained group therapist.

At the basis of all successful treatment is a relationship, with all its ramifications: transference, counter transference, rivalry, aloneness, gloom, happiness, confusion, discouragement, patience, dishonesty. It takes time, imagination, compassion, perseverance, and perhaps above all trust and hope to build any relationship that matters in a human life. To think for a moment that building a relationship with a child who has known little in his or her life of warmth, trust, hope and consistency from adults will be easy is wishful thinking. Raising a child is hard enough; effectively re-raising a child—emotionally and psychologically—in a treatment relationship, in ways which are inherently artificial compared to the normal growth of the human child, is very difficult. When the investment and return of investment in "your" child which make normal parenting possible in so many cases are not present, then an enormous amount of emotional stretching, giving and growing is required. We know of no way to insure that a relationship will happen between even the best intentioned therapist and the most willing child; we just know that if the relationship is not there, the odds are enormous that no effective treatment will take place.

In summary, there are four critical factors, as we see it, in determining the use of alternatives to institutionalization. First, the presence of compelling psychological and/or practical reasons for treatment; second, a thorough diagnosis to design a treatment plan in line with the realities of the situation and the child's needs; third, the presence within the community of a wide range of alternatives from which to choose; fourth, and perhaps most important, a growing bond between the individual child and the therapist which allows the building of the intimate emotional relationship necessary for any successful treatment.

Successful therapy is by its very nature a process which cannot be viewed as a method or recipe; like successful parenting and successful teaching, the variables are numerous and the reasons for success or failure often difficult to unravel even at times when one was part of the relationship. And we think that children and adolescents have a sixth sense which responds to the sensitivity of the dedicated therapist, teacher, child care worker, or other concerned adult.

Perhaps the ultimate protection, the ultimate reality which keeps a therapeutic relationship with a child honest is transference and countertransference. And it is often the tip off: someone who talks a good line, who seems to know about kids and treatment in the classroom or office or home, but who is physically uncomfortable, unapproachable, untouching, communicates a message; a strange kind of resistance in some of us doesn't allow us to touch in friendship or comfort when we don't truly care about children. The sad part of the increased awareness of sexual abuse of children is the newly self-conscious hesitation on the part of those who work with children: the child who once would have been hugged, in a moment of shared sorrow or happiness, may now go unhugged as the caregiver worries, not about his or her own motives, but about what others might be thinking or assuming. It will be a great loss if all open, spontaneous affection between children and adults comes to be viewed with suspicion.

Finally, then, we feel it is important for us to search out and develop as many alternatives as possible to the institutionalization of children, which in our opinion has almost always more negative side effects than positive value to children, their families, and the community at large. And we believe that alternatives sensitively tailored to the problems and needs of the individual child and entered into by a well trained and sensitive therapist with whom the child can develop a strong, intimate, trusting relationship have a good chance of being a helpful treatment and growth experience. To paraphrase Bruno Bettelheim, who said that "love is not enough"—the relationship alone is not enough—sensitivity and intuition alone are not enough—training and diagnostic skills and sound methods are not enough—but together, they ARE enough.

REFERENCES

Ackerly, W.C. (1967). Latency-age children who threaten or attempt to kill themselves. *Journal of the American Academy of Child Psychiatry*, 6, 242–261.

American Psychiatric Association. (1980). *Diagnostic and statistical manual of mental disorders. (3rd ed.)*.

Anderson, J.I. (1978). Order of difficulty in adult second language acquisition. In Ritchie, W.C. (Ed.), *Second language acquisition research*. New York: Academic Press.

Baker, K., & deKater, A. (1981). *Effectiveness of bilingual education: A review of the literature*. Washington: Office of Planning, Budget and Evaluation, U.S. Department of Education.

Barth, R.S. (1970). When children enjoy school. *Childhood Education*, January, 195–200.

Bettleheim, B. (1950). *Love is not enough: The treatment of emotionally disturbed children*. Glencove, Ill: Free Press.

Blumberg, M. (1981). Depression in abused and neglected children. *American Journal of Psychotherapy*, 35, 342–355.

Bowlby, J. (1960). Grief and mourning in infancy and early childhood. *Psychoanalytic Study of the Child*, 15, 9–52.

Bowlby, J. (1969). Disruption of affectional bonds and its effect on behaviour. *Canada's Mental Health Supplement*, 59, 12.

Brown, F. (1966). Childhood bereavement and subsequent psychiatric disorders. *British Journal of Psychiatry*, 112, 1035–1041.

Bruner, J. (1965). Growth of mind. *American Psychologist*, 20, 1007–1017.

Bruner, J. (1973). *Beyond the information given: Studies in the psychology of knowing*. New York: Norton.

Bruner, J., Jolly, A., & Sylva, K. (Eds.). *Play — Its role in development and evolution*. New York: Penguin.

Burke, R. (1984). *Economic recession and the quality of education: Some threatening trends*. Unpublished Manuscript, York University.

Cannon, G. (1966). Kindergarten class size: A study. *Childhood Education*, 43, 9–11.

Carins, R. B. (1983). The emergence of developmental psychology. In Mussen, P. (Ed.), *Handbook of child Psychology (Volume 1)*. New York: Wiley.

Case, R. (1983). *Intellectual development: A systematic reinterpretation*. New York: Academic Press.

Case, R. (1984). *The new stage theories in cognitive development: Why we need them, what they assert*. Paper presented at the Minnesota Symposium on Child Development.

Chomsky, N. (1972). *Language and mind (Enlarged edition).* San Diego, CA: Harcourt, Brace & Jovanovich.

Cohen, D.H. (1966). Dependency and class size. *Childhood Education, 43,* 9–11.

Cohen, S., & Willis, T.A. (1985). Stress, social support, and the buffering hypothesis. *Psychological Bulletin, 98,* 310–357.

Colbert, P., Newman, B., Ney, P. & Young, J. (1982). Learning disabilities as a symptom of depression in children. *Journal of Learning Disabilities, 15,* 333–336.

Cummins, J. (1978). The cognitive development of children in immersion programs. *Canadian Modern Language Review, 34,* 855–883.

Cummins, J. (1982). Through the looking glass: What really happens in an immersion classroom. *Interchange, 13,* 40–44.

Cummins, J., Swain, M., Nakajuma, K., Handscombe, J., Green, D. & Tran, C. (1982b). *Linguistic interdependence among Japanese and Vietnamese immigrant students.* Arlington, VA: National Clearinghouse for Bilingual Education.

Dale, P.S. (1976). *Language development: Structure and function. (2nd ed.).* New York: Holt, Rinehart & Winston.

Dearden, R.F. (1968). *The philosophy of primary education.* New York: Humanities Press.

DeLozier, P. (1982). Attachment theory and child abuse. In Parkes, C.M., & Stevenson-Hinde, J. (Eds.), *The place of attachment in human behavior.* New York: Basic Books.

Dewey, J. (1938). *Experience and education.* New York: Collier Books.

Dulay, H., & Burt, M. (1978). Creativity in language acquisition. In Ritchie, W.C. (Ed.), *Second language acquisition research.* New York: Academic Press.

Eckler, J. & Weininger, O. (1989). Structural parallels between pretend play and narratives. *Developmental Psychology, 25,* 736–743.

Ervin-Tripp, S. (1976). Studying the language of the child's milieu. In von Raffler-Engel, W., & Lebrun, Y. (Eds.), *Baby talk and infant speech.* Amsterdam: Swets & Zeitlinger.

Flavell, J. (1978). Comments. In Siegler, R.S. (Ed.), *Children's thinking: What develops?* Hillsdale, NJ: Lawrence Erlbaum.

Flavell, J. (1977). *Cognitive development.* Englewood Cliffs, NJ: Prentice-Hall.

Freud, A. (1953). A two-year-old goes to the hospital: Scientific film by James Roberston. *International Journal of Psychoanalysis, 34,* 284–287.

Freud, S. (1967). Mourning and melancholia. In Strachey, J. (Ed.), *The standard edition of the complete psychological works of Sigmund Freud (Vol. 14).* London: Hogarth.

Garbarino, J. (1977). The human ecology of child maltreatment: A conceptual model for research. *Journal of Marriage and the Family, 29,* 721–735.

Gardner, H. (1986, October). The Bilingual Blur. *New York Review of Books.*

Garvey, C. (1977). *Play.* Cambridge, MA: Harvard University Press.

Gary, J.O. (1978). Why speak if you don't need to? The case for a listening approach to beginning foreign language learning. In Ritchie, W.C. (Ed.), *Second language acquisition research.* New York: Academic Press.

Genesee, F. (1978). Scholastic effects on French immersion: An overview after ten years. *Interchange, 9,* 20–29.

Gibson, E.J., & Levin, H. (1975). *The psychology of reading.* Cambridge, MA: MIT Press.

Hakuta, K. (1986). *Mirror of language: The debate on bilingualism.* New York: Basic Books.

Hart, L. (1981). Classrooms are killing learning. *Principal, 60,* 8–11.

Hecaen, H. & Albert, M.L. (1978). *Human neuropsychology.* New York: Wiley.

Hoffer, B. (1976). Mexican-American acquisition of syntax. In von Raffler-Engel, W., & Lebrun, Y. (Eds.), *Baby talk and infant speech.* Amsterdam: Swets & Zeitlinger.

Ireland, D., Gunnell, K., & Santerre, L. (1981). *A study of the teaching and learning of aural/oral french in immersion classes.* Unpublished Manuscript.

Isaacs, S. (1930). *Intellectual growth in young children.* London: Routledge & Kegan Paul.

Isaacs, S. (1933). *Social development in young children.* London: Routledge & Sons.

Jackson, R.W.B. (1978). *Final report — Implications of declining enrolment for the schools of Ontario: A statement on effects and solutions.* Toronto: The Commission on Declining Enrolments in Ontario.

Katz, L. (1969, April). *Teaching in preschool: Roles and goals.* Address delivered at the Northern California Association for Education of Young Children.

Keller, M.B., Lanori, P.W., Rice, J., Coryell, W., & Hirschfield, R.M.A. (1986). The persistent risk of chronicity in recurrent episodes of nonbipolar major depressive disorder: A prospective follow-up. *American Journal of Psychiatry, 139,* 438–442.

Kessler, C. (1971). *The acquisition of syntax in bilingual children.* Washington, DC: Georgetown University Press.

Khanna, F. (1984). What's neo-Piagetian for preschoolers? *The Ontario Psychologist, 16,* 20–24.

King, N.R. (1979). The kindergartners' perspective. *Elementary School Journal, 80,* 81–87.

King, N.R. (1981). *Play in the workplace: Ethnographic perspectives on the construction of curriculum in classrooms.* Paper presented at the American Educational Research Association Annual Meeting.

Konorski, J. (1967). *Integrative activity of the brain.* Chicago: University of Chicago Press.

Krashen, S.D. (1978). Individual use of the monitor. In Ritchie, W.C. (Ed.), *Second language acquisition research.* New York: Academic Press.

LaPierre, L. (1978). *To herald a child: The report of the commission of inquiry into the education of the young child.* Toronto: AEFO, FWTAO, OECTA, OPSMTF.

Luria, A.R. (1966). *Higher cortical functions in man.* New York: Basic Books.

Luria, A.R. (1970). *Traumatic aphasia.* The Hague: Mouton & Co.

Luria, A.R. (1976). *Cognitive development — Its cultural and social foundations.* Cambridge, MA: Harvard University Press.

MacKinnon, C.E., Bordy, G.H., & Stoneman, Z. (1982). The effects of divorce on the home environments of preschool children. *Child Development, 53,* 1392–1399.

MacNamara, J. (1971). *The cognitive strategies of language learning.* Paper presented at the International Association of Applied Linguistics Conference on Child Language, Chicago.

Manitoba Association of School Trustees. (1976). The pupil teacher ratio question: Is there an answer? *MAST,* 3, 25–27.

Marris, P. (1985). *Widows and their families.* London: Routledge and Kegan Paul.

Marsh, L. (1970). *Alongside the child in primary school.* London: A & C Black.

Maruszewski, M. (1975). *Language communication and the brain—A neuropsychological study.* The Hague: Mouton.

McLaughlin, B.N. (1977). *Behavioral approaches to children with developmental delays.* St. Louis: Mosby. [Note: see text may be incorrect ref.]

Miller, D. R. & Swanson, G. E. (1960). *Inner conflict and defense,* New York, Holt.

Morgan, G.A.V. (1984). Yes! We should have bilingual immersion programs: A dialogue with Professor Weininger. *Interchange, 13*(2), 44–49.

Morris, M. (1978). *A study of childhood depression with special emphasis on classroom behaviours.* Unpublished doctoral dissertation. University of Toronto.

Morrissey, J.P., Klerman, L., & Goldman, H. (1980). *The enduring asylum: Cycles of institutional reform at Worchester State Hospital.* New York: Grune & Stratton.

Munn, J. (1978). Play therapy with a hockey game. *The Ontario Psychologist, 10,* 34–37.

Nahme-Huage, L., Singer, D., Singer, J., & Wheaton, A. (1977). Imaginative play training and perceptual motor interventions with emotionally disturbed hospitalized children. *American Journal of Orthopsychiatry, 47,* 238–249.

Ojemann, G.A., & Whitaker, H. (1978). The bilingual brain. *Archives of Neurology, 35,* 409–412.

Ontario Ministry of Education. (1975). *Education in the Primary and Junior Divisions.* Toronto, Canada.

Ontario Ministry of Education. (1980). *Issues and directions: The response to the final report of Commission on Declining School Enrolments in Ontario.* Toronto: Canada.

Ontario Ministry of Education. (1981). Bill 82: An act to amend the Education Act. Toronto, Canada.

Ontario Ministry of Education. (1986). Bill 30: Providing public funding for Catholic Schools. Toronto, Canada.

Ontario Ministry of Education. (1983). Heritage Language Legislation. A literature review. Toronto: Canada.

Panzicia, N. (1983). *Your teen and drugs.* Toronto: McGraw-Hill Ryerson.

Parmelee, A.H., Beckwith, L., Cohen, S.E., & Sigman, M. (1963). Social influences on infants at medical risk for behavioral difficulties. In Call, J.D., Galenson, E., & Tyson, R.L. (Eds.), *Frontiers of infant psychiatry.* New York: Basic Books.

Parry, G. (1982, April). *Paid employment, mental health, working class mothers.* Paper presented at the British Psychological Association, University of York.

Piaget, J. (1952). *The origins of intelligence in children.* New York: Norton.

Piaget, J. (1973). *The language and thought of the child.* New York: World.

Porwell, P. (1978). *Class size: A summary of research.* Arlington, VA: Educational Research Service.

Ridgway, L., & Lawton, I. (1968). *Family grouping in the primary school.* London: The Trinity Press.

Saltz, E., & Johnson, J. (1974). Training for thematic-fantasy play in culturally disadvantaged children: Preliminary results. *Journal of Educational Psychology, 66,* 623–360.

Scarfe, N.V. (1962). Play is education. *Childhood Education, 39,* 117–121.

Shapiro, S. (1975). Some classroom ABC'S: Research takes a closer look. *Elementary School Journal,* April 1975, 437–441.

Siegel, A.W., & Schadler, M. (1977). The development of young children's spatial representation of their classrooms. *Child Development, 43,* 388–394.

Smilansky, S. (1968). *The effects of sociodramatic play on disadvantaged preschool children.* New York: Wiley.

Snow, C. (1981). English speakers' acquisition of Dutch syntax. Native language and foreign language acquisition. *Annals of the New York Academy of Sciences, 379,* 235–250.

Sovner, R. & Hurley, A.D. (1983). The subjective experience of mentally retarded persons. *Psychiatric Aspects of Mental Retardation Newsletter, 2,* 41–42.

Spitz, R. (1945). Hospitalism: An inquiry into the genesis of psychiatric conditions in early childhood. *Psychoanalytic Study of the Child, 1,* 53–74.

Strain, P. & Weigernik, R. (1976). The effects of sociodramatic activities on social interaction among behaviorally disordered preschool children. *Journal of Special Education,* 10, 71–75.

Sund, R.B. (1974). Growing through sensitive listening and questioning. *Childhood Education,* November–December, 68–71.

Swain, M., & Lapkin, S. (1981). *Bilingual education in Ontario: A decade of research.* Toronto: Ministry of Education.

Tizard, B. (1974). Do social relationships affect language development? In Connolly, K., & Bruner, J., (Eds.), *Growth of Competence.* New York: Academic Press.

Tolman, E.D. (1984). Cognitive maps in rats and man. *Psychological Review, 55,* 189.

Toronto Board of Education. (1988). *Education of Black students in Toronto schools: Final report of the Consultative Committee.* Toronto, Canada.

Trad, P. (1987). *Infant and childhood depression: Developmental factors.* New York: Wiley.

United States Supreme Court. (1974). Lau vs. Nichols.

Valenzuela, M. (1989). *Mother-infant attachment, developmental status and quality of home care in young chronically undernourished children.* Unpublished Ph.D. dissertation, University of Toronto, Toronto, Canada.

Vygostky, L.S. (1962). *Thought and language.* Cambridge, MA: MIT Press.

Weininger, O. (1975). The disabled and dying children: Why does it have to hurt so much? *Ontario Psychologist, 7,* 29–35.

Weinginer, O. (1979). *Play & education: The basic tool for early childhood learning.* Springfield, Illinois: Charles C Thomas.

Weininger, O. (1981). A neurological base to understanding second language development. *Teacher Education, 18,* 70–89.

Weininger, O. (1984). Educating the child for the year 2001. *The Ontario Psychologist, 16,* 3–7.

Weininger, O. (1984b). *The clinical psychology of Melanie Klein.* Springfield, Illinois: Charles C Thomas.

Weininger, O. (1986). *The differential diagnostic technique: A visual motor projective test.* Springfield, Ill: Charles C Thomas.

Weininger, O. (1989). *Children's phantasies: The shaping of relationships.* London: Karnac.

Weininger, O., & Muskat, J.J. (1978). Madison Avenue School: offering hope for troubled children. *Orbit, 42,* 15–17.

Weininger, O., Rotenberg, G., & Henry, A. (1972). Body image of handicapped children. *Journal of Personality Assessment, 36,* 248–253.

Wells, G. (1978). What makes for successful language development? In Campbell, R.N., & Smith, P.T. (Eds.), *Recent advances in the psychology of language.* New York: Plenum.

Wells, G. (1982, February). Address given at the Ontario Institute for Studies in Education.

Whitaker, J.A. (1978). Bilingualism: A neurolinguistics perspective. In Ritchie, W.C. (Ed.), *Second language acquisition research.* New York: Academic Press.

Willig, A. & H.F. Greenberg. (Eds.) (1986). *Bilingualism and learning disabilities: Policy and practice for teachers and administrators.* New York: American Library.

Willig, A. (1985). A meta-analysis of selected studies on the effectiveness of bilingual education. *Review of Educational Research, 15,* 269–317.

Wilson, R. & Conock, M. (1982). *An assessment of the 50/50 programme in the English sector schools.* Ottawa: The Ottawa Roman Catholic Separate School Board.

Winnicott, D.W. (1965). *The family and individual development.* London: Tavistock Publication.

Winokur, G., Cadoret, R., Dorzab, J., & Baker, M. (1971). Depressive disease: A genetic study. *Archives of General Psychiatry, 24,* 135–144.

Wolfe, D.A. (1985). Child abusive parents: An empirical review and analysis. *Psychological Bulletin, 97,* 462–482.

Wright, E., Shapson, S., Eason, G., & Fitzgerald, J. (1977). *Effects of class size in the junior grades: A study.* Toronto: Ontario Department of Education.

Yakolev, D. & Lecours, A. (1967). The myelogenetic cycles of regional maturation of the brain. In Minkowski, (Ed.), *Regional development of the brain in early life: Symposium.* Philadelphia: F.A. Davis.

Zarzour, K. (1986, March 26). *Update on french immersion education.* Toronto Star, Toronto, Canada.

INDEX